Access your Online Resources

Transforming Your Tutor Time Curriculum is accompanied by a number of printable online materials, designed to ensure this resource best supports your professional needs.

Go to https://resourcecentre.routledge.com/speechmark and click on the cover of this book.

Answer the question prompt using your copy of the book to gain access to the online content.

"I was a form tutor for five years with the same group and it was one of my happiest professional experiences. However, I remember asking the senior leader in charge of professional learning if there were any courses or support or books I could use in order to make sure I was as effective as possible in my tutor role. He didn't know of any, and it was left at that. How I could have done with Kirsten Colquhoun's 'Transforming your Tutor Time Curriculum'! It's beautifully researched, overflowing with ideas and above all makes the case for ensuring a rich, robust and nurturing experience for our young people in tutor time."

– **Mary Myatt**, Education Writer and Speaker

"Kirsten's book makes a compelling case for the crucial importance of Tutor Time. She gives practical, balanced, actionable suggestions to ensure it is thoughtfully planned and intentionally structured. The book, which is underpinned by Kirsten's considerable professional experience and her secure understanding of what the relevant research evidence has to say, should be invaluable for Tutor Teachers working with pupils of all ages and in all contexts."

– **Dr Jill Berry**, Former Head Teacher, Author, Education Consultant

"Insightful and practical, this guide redefines tutor time as a powerful opportunity to strengthen school culture and improve outcomes."

– **Dr Carl Hendrick**, Academica University of Applied Sciences

"A wonderfully engaging book for teachers – full of insight and practical examples – that illuminates how a little dedicated time with pupils at the start of the school day can have a profound impact."

– **Henry Hepburn**, Scotland editor, Tes

"It's hard to imagine a more thorough and thoughtful guide to making the most effective use of tutor time. Colquhoun's book is very well supported with research evidence from psychology and beyond, and it should feature in any CPD library."

– **Dr Jonathan Firth**, University of Strathclyde

"Kirsten Colquhoun has set out a clear, interesting, and evidence-informed approach which will expand your understanding, develop your practice and enhance pupil experiences. The book is a must-read for teachers and educationalists alike."

– **Dr Barry Black**, Educational Researcher

"Kirsten Colquhoun's *Transforming Your Tutor Time Curriculum* is nothing short of a revelation. In a time when schools are facing increasing pressures: rising mental health challenges, concerns over student engagement and the need to foster belonging—this book offers a lifeline. It's not just a guide; it's an invitation to reimagine what tutor time can achieve."

– **Dr Haili Hughes**

Transforming Your Tutor Time Curriculum

This accessible book is a trusted companion for every teacher who has found themselves in charge of a tutor group. Inside, you'll find a treasure trove of activities that require little to no planning but will have a positive and engaging impact on your pupils.

Bursting with creativity and actionable tips, the book recognises the myriad demands on a teacher's time and is centred around making tutor time meaningful and giving students the best start to the day. Divided into three key sections – School Culture and Community, Health and Wellbeing and Academic Improvement – a variety of activities are provided, each with helpful background context as well as clear instructions and discussion prompts. The activities cover diverse topics, from SEND (special educational needs and disabilities) support to forming habits, and will create a tutor time curriculum which strengthens your understanding of each pupil in your care and facilitates positive relationships and support among students and staff.

Transforming your Tutor Time Curriculum is an essential resource for teachers looking for concrete tutor group guidance, as well as heads of year and pastoral and Personal, Social, Health Education (PSHE) leads. It is also valuable reading for senior leaders who would like to think more strategically about the low-cost, high-impact benefits of tutor time.

Kirsten Colquhoun is a dedicated educator with over 15 years of experience in secondary education. Originally graduating as a history teacher, she has since earned an MEd specialising in pastoral care, providing her with a broad perspective and a critical understanding of pupil wellbeing. Her ongoing work in schools ensures she remains deeply connected to the realities of classroom dynamics, enabling her to blend practical insight and experience with academic expertise.

Transforming Your Tutor Time Curriculum

100+ Activities to Support Wellbeing, Strengthen Culture and Supercharge Success

Kirsten Colquhoun

Taylor & Francis Group

LONDON AND NEW YORK

Designed cover image: Getty Images

First published 2025
by Routledge
4 Park Square, Milton Park, Abingdon, Oxon OX14 4RN

and by Routledge
605 Third Avenue, New York, NY 10158

Routledge is an imprint of the Taylor & Francis Group, an informa business

© 2025 Kirsten Colquhoun

The right of Kirsten Colquhoun to be identified as author of this work has been asserted in accordance with sections 77 and 78 of the Copyright, Designs and Patents Act 1988.

All rights reserved. The purchase of this copyright material confers the right on the purchasing institution to photocopy or download pages which bear the support material icon and a copyright line at the bottom of the page. No other parts of this book may be reprinted or reproduced or utilised in any form or by any electronic, mechanical, or other means, now known or hereafter invented, including photocopying and recording, or in any information storage or retrieval system, without permission in writing from the publishers.

Trademark notice: Product or corporate names may be trademarks or registered trademarks, and are used only for identification and explanation without intent to infringe.

British Library Cataloguing-in-Publication Data
A catalogue record for this book is available from the British Library

ISBN: 978-1-032-99882-4 (hbk)
ISBN: 978-1-032-99879-4 (pbk)
ISBN: 978-1-003-60651-2 (ebk)

DOI: 10.4324/9781003606512

Typeset in Optima
by Apex CoVantage, LLC

Access the Support Material: https://resourcecentre.routledge.com/speechmark

This book is dedicated to Alice, who was most surprised when the first one was not.

For all the things my hands have held, the best by far is you.

Contents

Acknowledgements		xii
Foreword		xiii
	Introduction	**1**
PART I	LOGISTICS OF TUTOR TIME	16
PART II	DESIGNING A TUTOR TIME CURRICULUM	36
PART III	TUTOR TIME FOR SUPPORTING SCHOOL CULTURE AND COMMUNITY	44
PART IV	TUTOR TIME FOR HEALTH AND WELLBEING	101
PART V	TUTOR TIME FOR ACADEMIC IMPROVEMENT	132
	Final thoughts	**161**
References		163
Index		166

Acknowledgements

A huge thank you to Grant, who has perfected the art of enabling my many plots, plans and projects while not asking me too many questions. You deserve a medal, or at least another round of golf.

I'm also incredibly grateful to the loving Emma, whose dedication to staying in touch and making me laugh may have made the book-writing process longer, but certainly more entertaining.

Thank you to Harriet and George for your wonderful company during long writing sessions.

And to my mum, for the proofreading that has almost compensated for my second-rate spelling abilities.

Foreword

Education is the beating heart of our society, and as teachers, we have the unique privilege – and responsibility – of shaping futures. Yet, amidst the bustling days filled with lesson plans, assessments and pastoral care, there lies a golden opportunity that too often goes underutilised: tutor time.

Kirsten Colquhoun's *Transforming Your Tutor Time Curriculum* is nothing short of a revelation. In a time when schools are facing increasing pressures: rising mental health challenges, concerns over student engagement and the need to foster belonging – this book offers a lifeline. It's not just a guide; it's an invitation to reimagine what tutor time can achieve.

Colquhoun captures the essence of what we, as teachers, often feel but struggle to articulate: that those 15–20 minutes each day are not filler but foundational. Done well, tutor time can act as the glue that binds school culture, academic success and student wellbeing into a cohesive whole. This book doesn't just highlight its importance. It equips us with over 100 creative, research-informed activities to transform these moments into a powerhouse of connection and growth.

What makes this book truly remarkable is how deeply it understands the realities of school life. It doesn't shy away from the challenges we face as teachers. Instead, it meets us where we are, with practical, actionable strategies which honour the constraints of time and resources, while igniting a renewed sense of purpose.

Whether it's fostering a sense of belonging in a new Year 7 cohort, supporting the emotional resilience of students preparing for exams, or simply giving them a moment to breathe and reflect, this book is packed with ideas that resonate deeply with every teacher's mission.

I found myself nodding in agreement as I read, reminded of my own experiences as both a classroom teacher and form teacher. The activities in this book are more than just tools; they're conversation starters, community builders and, ultimately, pathways to helping young people thrive.

Foreword

For senior leaders, this book offers a strategic framework to align tutor time with wider school improvement goals. For teachers, it's a treasure trove of ideas that will inspire and energise. For students, it's a quiet promise: that their voices matter, that their needs are seen and that the time we spend together each morning or afternoon can set the tone for everything that follows.

In Kirsten's capable hands, tutor time becomes more than a daily routine – it becomes a transformative practice. Her passion for education shines through every page, making this an essential read for anyone committed to creating schools where students and staff alike can flourish.

I feel privileged to introduce this book to you, and I can't wait to see the ripple effects it will have in classrooms across the country. I loved being a form teacher and I also love bumping into ex-students who always speak fondly of our time together. When we invest in moments of connection, the impact lasts a lifetime.

Dr Haili Hughes
Academica University of Applied Sciences
Director of Education at IRIS Connect

Introduction

Amazon founder Jeff Bezos commented recently that he is regularly asked to predict the future of businesses. Time and again in media interviews journalists attempt to elicit his wisdom on such matters. Instead, he suggests that it is far more sensible for him – and others – to focus on what we know won't change. For Amazon, that is their reliability, good value and fast delivery – the things that don't change and are valued by his customers – and this is where he believes his focus should remain, on the important foundations of good business and not be drawn in by a desire to predict the next big thing.

Within education, we can learn from this approach. All too often political forces, media attention and almost anyone with an opinion wants to know how schools will respond to myriad contemporary issues from environmental challenges to energy drinks consumption and deliver outstanding academic results at the same time! Schools have to be many things to many people; just designing the timetable for a busy secondary school is a bit like playing extreme sudoku, and delivering it requires teachers to spin a vast array of plates every day! School leaders are under immense pressure to balance the books, continually improve and ensure quality experiences for their learners. We just have to google 'school news' to see the vast array of concerning searches: wellbeing and mental health concerns, increasing concerns regarding school exclusions, teacher shortages, missed attainment targets and so on. In such a climate, schools, authorities, parents and just about anyone with an opinion consistently voice their concerns. It seems, given half the chance, external pressures would have educators pulled in a thousand different directions each day, often to the detriment of focusing on the key priorities of what we know to be true – *a good education has the power to change lives.*

And so this book considers the approach of Jeff Bezos and focuses on one of the core facets of success rather than looking for shiny novel approaches.

So we start right at the beginning of the school day and aim to support consistency, relationships and good systems to help maintain excellent school outcomes.

What is tutor time?

Form, registration, homeroom, tutor time, house sessions, and even clan time; it goes by many different names but it is a central and enduring feature of most school days. Done well, it can act as the foundation to support wellbeing, school culture and positive outcomes for all young people. For the basis of this book, we will refer to this session as tutor time, often the first session of the day, and sometimes the first session of the afternoon, where pupil attendance is recorded, information is shared and a host of different activities take place. The teachers delivering this session will be referred to as tutor teachers.

These sessions should be recognised as bridges, or transition points between the home lives of our pupils, and to their school life. It has huge potential to support pupils, echo key school messages and improvements and with careful planning we can maximise its impact and reach. Tutor time is a rare time in the day when pupils are given space and support to prepare for that daily transition: for all pupils this is helpful, for some essential, and it is worth noting that pupils' individual needs will vary and change throughout their school careers. Daily time together before the core activities of school begin is a wonderful opportunity to set pupils up for a successful day, support the wider aims of school improvement and provide pupils with a solid foundation on which to build their experiences and school success. At the core of all tutor time is the primary need to account for and ensure pupils are registered, but done right, tutor time offers a huge potential beyond simple registers and paperwork.

In seeking improvement, we must be guided by the research and supported to seek solutions which extend beyond 'feeling good'. Our efforts should be directed towards practices and solutions that deliver tangible results. One such area of focus is ensuring pupils' sense of belonging is explored and supported. Pupils need their social needs met to fully engage in their academic pursuits. Implementing effective school systems, such as prioritising well-structured tutor time, can contribute significantly to enhancing pupil belonging and fostering positive outcomes.

Introduction

Tutor time is a vehicle for ensuring a secure pupil–staff relationships are established, for supporting a wider system of safeguarding and monitoring pupil attendance. Tutor time can support pupils in gaining skills and confidence and, crucially, it enables schools to fulfil a number of legislative requirements, from group worship to effective attendance records and delivery of key messages.

This book will consider different themes which can be explored during tutor time, as well as different approaches, and will offer a treasure trove of easy ideas to help busy teachers maximise the impact and effectiveness of this time. The information which follows in the chapters ahead aims to marry the research, theory and practice together to create a resource to support teachers and schools. Daniel Willingham (2012) stresses the importance of teachers being informed by research rather than strictly guided by it, contrasting with the approach of medical or scientific professionals. He suggests that teachers adopt a mind-set akin to that of architects, acknowledging the diverse needs and outcomes expected by various stakeholders, parents, pupils, communities and teachers themselves. I recommend approaching the upcoming chapters with this perspective, well-intentioned yet mindful of the nuances that require consideration before applying them universally in your unique school, environment and community. In an era where we often have over-information, exercising caution and thoughtful consideration is crucial before making any changes or adaptations. This book has been written with the intention of aiding schools and teachers in their quest to ensure tutor time enhances the overall experience and quality of school for young people.

The role of a tutor teacher has changed and developed over the years and yet it is often ill defined. Tutor time ensures that attendance can be managed and recorded effectively, and more recently has evolved to be something many recognise as First Line Guidance with increasingly pastoral care. One of the biggest complaints from teachers I spoke with is that the role and duties of a tutor teacher are seldom discussed or provided for during professional learning events, rarely trained for and, often, consequently undervalued. Teachers commented that this was frustrating and hindered their ability to maximise the impact they could have during this time.

The role is an appendage, added onto a teacher's vast responsibilities, whether or not they actively seek it, or welcome it. With a lack of guidance for the role, no exams or measurable outcomes, requirements or a wider sense of value, tutor time can be a less formal element of school life. This can lead to it being treated as an afterthought, lacking in specific consideration or training. In my research it was clear that teachers actively desire more guidance, support and dedicated time for this additional responsibility so that they can perform the role well. However, overcrowded curriculums, lack of time and funding, as well as busy duties as a subject teacher, often leave little room for such tasks. It is crucial that we address this issue. Recognising the different titles schools assign to this role, it is clear that there is a wide variety of approaches to training, consistency, recognition and support for teachers. Therefore, read on and let this book act as a companion to help you in this role.

Enhancing your skills as a tutor teacher

Teacher Tapp, an app, has frequently featured questions about tutor time, helpfully proving comparative responses. For those of you who haven't heard about Teacher Tapp, you're missing out! In 2017, Professor Becky Allen and Laura McInerney developed a survey app designed to engage teachers in answering brief, daily questions about various topics related to education. Initially, they aimed to explore whether teachers who had their own classroom were more positively influenced to remain in the profession. While their hypothesis was disproved, the initiative revealed the importance of consulting teachers' opinions and insights on matters affecting their profession. Teacher Tapp was created to address the gap in involving teachers in decision-making processes within education and has since become a platform for empowering educators by amplifying our voices. It boasts a wealth of interesting findings. Helpfully, it regularly repeats questions asked to generate comparative data samples. A discussion on X (previously known as Twitter) sparked by one of the findings inspired me to make the jump to write this book.

I was motivated to write this book also due to a number of professional discussions, realisation of the demand for tutor time resources, training and support. This, along with a body of research and years of experience, has been a driving factor in deciding what to incorporate in the pages ahead.

In October 2023, more than 5000 teachers participated in providing feedback on Teacher Tapp. Among the respondents, 61% reported that they meet with their tutor group at the beginning of the day, primarily for registration purposes.

Additional questions in February 2024 confirmed that 20% of over 6000 teachers reported spending 16–20 minutes daily with their tutor group, representing the most frequent response. Notably, 40% of teachers dedicate more than 21 minutes per day to their tutor group. These statistics shed light on the varying approaches to tutor time, underscoring the significance of this data. The substantial number of teachers contributing to these findings reaffirms the value and relevance of such insights.

The feedback and findings from the Teacher Tapp prompted discussion within teacher Twitter circles which further revealed inconsistency in approaches to this crucial role. Across schools, there exists a wide disparity in time allocation, titles, expectations and processes, sometimes even within the same institution. Nevertheless, tutor time remains a permanent fixture, and its significance in fostering positive expectations, safeguarding measures and relationships is becoming increasingly paramount. As Jeff Bezos suggests, it is essential to concentrate on the elements that remain constant. Therefore, amidst the myriad pressures educators face, including OFSTED evaluations, technological advancements, challenges in meeting special educational needs and disabilities (SEND), educational reforms, behavioural issues, teacher shortages, and numerous other stressors, let us prioritise supporting students in experiencing a positive start to their day.

As the responsibilities of tutor teachers have expanded, more classroom teachers find themselves shouldering frontline guidance roles, including managing pupil friendships, processing learning referrals, implementing first stage interventions and other tasks, which they may not always embrace. Fitting the many aims of school into what is a relatively short academic year, and day, can be a challenge. Tutor time is unique to the rest of the school day in that there are rarely prescribed curriculums to deliver and fewer deadlines to meet. Tutor time can be unaccounted for and often free for year heads and tutors to plan as they see fit.

However, this can be a double-edged sword. The fullness and richness of the rest of the day places huge burden on teachers, who are often balancing many demands. In prioritising these many demands, tutor time activities, especially those without a long-term strategic goal, can understandably be overlooked, especially during pressure points in the year, for example ahead of preliminary exams, coursework deadlines, report writing and final exam deadlines.

Many teachers frequently express concern about the insufficient training provided for these additional duties. Juggling competing demands such as delivering the curriculum, marking and addressing the diverse needs of parents, students, administrators and local authorities often leaves teachers feeling overstretched in terms of both time and resources. With this in mind, and with a huge respect for your time and expertise, this book presents you with an excellent opportunity to enhance your skills. At the very least, it aims to provide you with ideas for tutor time that can be readily implemented without overly encroaching on your precious time.

What quickly became clear from my research is the value many teachers, leaders and school communities place on effective tutor time. Senior leaders who acknowledge the vital importance of starting the day well, and spoke positively about using tutor time to disseminate key messages to pupils, reiterate expectations in a setting where there is greater accountability compared to large assemblies. Pupils were also keen to discuss the positives of tutor time: they recognised the importance of having a consistent session with the same teacher each day, as did many parents who value the interaction between a member of staff who knows their child to the vital safeguarding information that accurate registration taking enables, and to the teachers who frequently commented, happily, that it was the one period of the day not timetabled, over-packed or outcome-driven.

Supporting pupils' emotional and academic wellbeing

The nature of education has evolved significantly over the last few decades; schools are increasingly tasked with responding to the social, health and emotional needs of pupils as well as being concerned with their academic progress. More and more there is concern about attendance rates with an ever-increasing number of young people providing reasons for avoiding school. Fortunately, we have both a responsive and proactive school system which, with careful planning, adequate resources and support, is well positioned to respond to many of these pressures.

Take, for example, the success of school-based initiatives such as Childsmile that demonstrate the significantly positive impact schools can and do have in supporting public health interventions. The Childsmile initiative in Scotland is a national program aimed at improving the oral health of children.

Childsmile was developed from two national trials in 2006–2008. Research revealing the shocking numbers of children under the age of 6 suffering from tooth decay promoted this intervention. The initiatives positively responded to this issue with the aim to reduce numbers and improve overall oral health

Introduction

for young children. Childsmile focuses on providing preventative dental care and education to children from birth to age 12, as well as pregnant women and their families. The initiative offers a range of services which are delivered in partnership between local health boards and schools. Services include supervised tooth brushing in schools and nurseries, fluoride varnish applications, and oral health promotion activities to target parents. It even provides toothpaste and brushes to young children across Scotland. Childsmile has successfully reduced dental decay and promotes lifelong oral health habits among children in Scotland.

There are no sections of this book suggesting you start a tooth brushing initiative but this initiative serves as evidence and hopefully inspiration that through embedded processes and support we can and do make a huge difference. The effectiveness of this initiative rests on the partnerships established between local authorities and schools, funding, resources and the perceived value it has. What we learn from this success story is the significant power schools have in promoting and supporting healthy behaviours both in school and in wider life when they operate cohesively for positive outcomes.

Despite the huge demands on our education system, resources and time, teachers and schools across the country demonstrate a commitment to improving the lives of our young people, but it is challenging. Ask any teacher, pupil or person working in a school and they will tell you, it is a busy day with a huge amount of variety and demands on teachers and pupils alike. Pupils in secondary education will take a variety of subjects and no two days are ever the same. During this busy day, it is quite unlikely that students will see the same teacher more than once, but rather each teacher will see different pupils, period by period. This system has a huge variety of benefits for young people. Having a breadth of subject choices maximises the chances of a pupil finding a subject they enjoy, while equipping them with a wide range of skills and a deep knowledge of different disciplines. These are hugely positive attributes to any curriculum.

However unlike primary school, the secondary school system means that within the day pupils have a wider variety of teachers so they do not have consistent contact with a main teacher who knows them and the bigger picture of them as a learner. This can make the challenges of supporting learners very difficult. It is harder for individual teachers – in the business of the day – to spot changes in their pupils, notice differences in their behaviours and subtle indications that they may need support. The guidance and pastoral systems in schools have been designed with this in mind, but again the business of the day means that pupils may not have daily contact with their pastoral lead. However we know that this change in relationship is hard for young people, they mourn the loss of a consistent teacher who knows them, and most likely also knows the name of their pets and various other details. In their 2019 study, Jindal-Snape and Cantali explored the significant shift students undergo when transitioning from primary to secondary school, particularly focusing on the loss of the primary teacher relationship. In primary school, pupils often have a single teacher who understands them holistically, providing consistent emotional and academic support. However, in secondary school, students encounter a system with multiple subject-specific teachers, which can disrupt the close, supportive relationships they previously experienced.

The loss of this relationship can profoundly impact pupils' emotional and academic wellbeing. The secure and supportive environment fostered by a primary teacher often serves as a vital anchor for students. When this is lost, students may experience anxiety, uncertainty and a decreased sense of school connectedness and engagement. Therefore, it is crucial for secondary school teachers to recognise the importance of fostering strong, positive relationships with their pupils, especially during their first year. This support can help mitigate the challenges of this significant educational transition, aiding in the students' overall wellbeing and academic success, once again underpinning the crucial role of a tutor.

Making tutor time meaningful

Within British schools, as in many other parts of the world, there are clearly defined roles for pastoral leads which have been in place since the 1970s. Responsibility and authority is given to year heads, heads of guidance and designated pastoral leaders. These leadership structures ensure personal, social and health education are effectively delivered; that safeguarding practices are in place; and that there is a connection between the education sector and the external agencies that play a role in keeping children and young people safe.

As this system has developed, many schools and authorities have aptly assessed the need to ensure tutor teachers are active in their role as frontline guidance supporting the vital work of pastoral leads, acting as a daily and consistent adult in place to support and monitor the young people in their form in a short, daily contact session. Pastoral leads play a vital role but may go days without seeing individual pupils. Pastoral leads may deliver the PSE curriculum and will be responsible to pupils who need support. With a sizeable caseload it is rarely possible for guidance staff to have routine daily contact with all of the pupils in their care and so a tutor time system which enables other teachers to step into this role is invaluable.

We are fortunate in the UK that all four of our home nations have excellent legislation to outline the crucial roles schools play in ensuring the safeguarding and wellbeing of our young people. Yet so much of it is open to interpretation, for example, our constructs for assessing wellbeing are often based on externally composed frameworks or indicators, and require noticing differences and changes in pupils – for example, a teacher who has daily contact with a pupil will be better placed to notice a change in their interests, or conversely a withdrawal from activities which might indicate further issues. Ensuring the role of a tutor teacher is respected and protected is vital for ensuring positive pupil outcomes.

This consistency also promotes efficiency by streamlining processes and maximising instructional time, allowing for a greater focus on teaching and learning. Additionally, routines contribute to a sense of belonging and community within the school, as everyone follows similar procedures, fostering unity and cohesion. Rules, uniform, celebrations and notices can be transmitted at the same time across multiple year groups, creating a system to enforce school norms, support behaviour management strategies and support pupils to get off on a positive foot for the day. Missing equipment, uniforms or issues can be dealt with before they creep into the classroom and disrupt learning activities, and this is good news for everyone. A more detailed approached can be found on page 64.

Media headlines commonly highlight the myriad challenges schools face, including increased behavioural issues, a rise in attendance issues heightened student anxiety. However, one area that received less attention is the impact of the pandemic on pupil social skills.

Through tutor time we can provide pupils with a preparation zone, somewhere pupils can adjust before the day's learning begins. Creating a space where students have the time and crucial support to readjust to the school environment is not only highly effective but also vital for some students. Tutor time provides that gentle transition between outside life and school, helping all students prepare for the day ahead. Importantly, it also supports neurodiverse students in navigating school life.

Tutor time also helps communicate and underpin the wider values of the school community. This can be done through the sharing of values and discussions relating to and challenges, changes or developments in school rules, values and structure. It offers space and guidance to reflect on previous behaviour and actively plan together for improvement. Tutor time ensures that attendance can be managed and recorded effectively, later evolving to be something many refer to as First Line Guidance. Humans crave connections, it is what has sustained us as a species and creating time for this is essential for mental and academic wellbeing. Having a morning meeting with a teacher who may not be your subject teacher also supports and develops pupil–staff relationships and ensures they have a central person they can go to for day-to-day information and support.

Furthermore, through the establishment of proper routines pupils learn valuable life skills such as timekeeping, discipline, organisation and social skills. These attributes all support a positive school community and are crucial for academic success and personal development. By adhering to established routines, pupils also experience reduced worry and stress levels, as predictability helps alleviate uncertainty and cognitive load and promotes a sense of calm. Overall, establishing a positive tutor time system can play a vital role in shaping positive school cultures by promoting consistency, relationship efficiency, community, self-discipline and wellbeing.

How to use this book

Imagine as an adult having access to a dedicated personal assistant, one who regularly checks in on you, helps you prepare for the day ahead, ensures you have everything you need, keeps you updated with any necessary information and kindly welcomes you to your workplace each day. You can be certain that you'd be less likely to forget essentials like your door pass, lunch or diary, or find yourself rushing during breaks to grab snacks you wish you had remembered! You'd perhaps be more able to get on with tasks with a more stable mental load. You may find yourself more organised and better able to respond to myriad tasks and challenges each working day presents. This level of care and attention makes a significant difference. It's not just about convenience; it's about fostering a sense of security and support.

After graduating with a history degree, my decision to pursue teaching as a career was fuelled by my eagerness to share my love for history. I could think of few other outlets where I would have a willing audience and a chance to talk about the topics and subjects I loved all day long.

During my university years, I had been fortunate to have an inspiring and luminary mentor, Professor McIvor, who embodied everything I aspired to be as a history teacher: knowledgeable, great wisdom and a captivating storyteller capable of transporting us students to different historical eras. He introduced the past in a way that cultivated empathy, understanding and intrigue. The narratives he created left me inspired and eager for more. I consciously wanted to be like him and I aimed to emulate his teaching style believing that he had hit the jackpot of jobs.

However much I had planned for my career in education, I see now that I failed to fully consider what a comprehensive teaching day within a secondary school would actually incorporate, compared to that of a university day! My naivety led me to believe it would be similar to what I had experienced at university where students (who had specifically opted in) would willingly engage and shaping young minds with my inspirational tales of days gone by would be easy.

Of course, teacher training was a baptism of fire where my attention was directed towards crafting lesson plans, delivering instructions within the classroom setting and managing behaviour. I quickly came to realise that the responsibilities of a teacher reach well beyond the boundaries of academic curriculum and the physical confines of the classroom walls, often influenced by factors beyond my control. As educators, a substantial part of our role is dedicated to the broader objectives of education: equipping students for the challenges of the real world, aiding them in making positive decisions, supporting inclusion and equality and nurturing their cultural heritage for societal success after school. This essential work extends beyond traditional lesson delivery.

After getting a more of a grasp of the academic curriculum which was prescribed by exam boards, or more senior members of staff, I turned my attention to all the many other tasks my role as a teacher demanded. What I hadn't fully appreciated before is the degree of autonomy and responsibility teachers have in shaping pupils' experiences beyond the specified academic curriculum. We have the freedom to design co-curricular and super-curricular activities, enrichment courses and tutor time activities that can be highly motivating for both pupils and staff. However, this autonomy also comes with the challenge of balancing competing demands and priorities within busy school environments.

In my research, the vast majority of teachers stated that there was no formal guidance for tutor time in their schools. In many cases, teachers are left to exercise their own judgement in determining how to spend this time. While this can be empowering, it also means that the responsibility for designing and implementing these activities falls squarely on the shoulders of individual teachers. This can be demanding, especially when faced with time constraints and pressure to meet the vast array obligations comprising all teachers' remits within schools.

Navigating this balance between autonomy and responsibility can be challenging and akin to walking a tightrope! So this book acknowledges that while we may have boundless passion for our subject, we may feel less adept at developing other aspects of our role. Within the busy, packed curriculum there is a safety net of tasks, aims and outcomes. Being a tutor teacher can feel very much removed from this, it is daunting, especially when you consider each session in isolation – How do you fill 20 minutes each day? What *will* you do with 30 pupils every. single. morning?

Considering tutor time as a standalone daily activity can make it seem more difficult to tie into other areas of school life. It is well worth considering your weekly routines, termly aims and annual expectations for tutor time. Or even better if you have a year head to offer support to do this in line with wider school aims. Whatever approach you take, this book hopes to offer you timesaving ideas and alleviate some of the burdensome elements of planning tutor time. This is especially crucial in educational settings, where the wellbeing and success of young people are paramount. The concept of tutor time plays a pivotal role in creating this supportive environment within schools. It ensures that various components of the school system work together seamlessly. In the wellbeing section, we will consider a variety of strategies for approaching tutor time effectively, recognising its importance in nurturing a positive and cohesive school community.

For a number of reasons, it is well worth considering embedding a structure into your weekly tutor time routines and setting specific tasks and activities on specific days. Ideally this should come from whomever is in charge of the school's strategic improvements and should, ideally, reflect the priorities and plans for the school community. Although delivered by an array of teachers, tutor time will not be reflective of the individual teacher's set of aims, ideals and curriculum and so it needs to be based on something else. Ideally the wider aims and priorities of the school should filter in here to provide an overarching structure.

Even having a basic skeleton will help with planning and gives a sense of purpose to the sessions. It also creates certainty for our learners and acts as means to minimise the amount of planning required while removing the mental burden of day-to-day planning. It also helps create norms as pupils have a clearer sense of what is coming on different days. Creating and sustaining routines and norms in the classroom is a key strategy to support positive behaviour and relieve cognitive burdens. Of course, this may well adapt and change throughout different times of the year when pupils may require different focuses.

For example, many of the tutors we spoke to felt it was important to do a 'fun' task on a Friday. This typically came in the tutor form of a quiz or challenge, and ideally these tasks would support the social focus and aims of tutor time as well. Others had to organise activities around assembly days which were often fixed to specific days of the week, leaving four days to fill.

There is no right or wrong way to organise your week, there is just what works for you, your school and your pupils. Following the essential administrative work, which mainly comprises registration, processing known absences, passing on medical notes and following up similar issues directly with pupils, my own routine went something like this:

Monday	Community or school culture focus
Tuesday	Wellbeing
Wednesday	Assembly – whole school or religious observations
Thursday	Connections to the wider community – annual celebrations
Friday	Academic competencies or study reviews

With that in mind, this book is divided into five key areas.

Part I Logistics of tutor time

This essential section provides a thorough exploration of both the conceptual and logistical aspects of tutor time, offering a comprehensive guide for educators to understand its purpose, structure and implementation. It examines key questions such as the how, why and where of tutor time, as well as the potential impacts of its absence on school culture and pupil outcomes.

Readers are guided through detailed sections that encourage critical reflection on how tutor time fits into their curriculum, including considerations around its duration, scheduling and overall organisation. The section also addresses practical elements such as record-keeping and monitoring attendance, highlighting their importance in ensuring tutor time runs effectively and meets its objectives.

Beyond logistics, this section explores broader concepts such as the use of physical spaces for tutor time, the application of field theory to enhance its purpose and the challenges posed by SEND needs and cognitive load management. Additionally, it provides insight into alternative arrangements for schools seeking flexibility and even examines what a school environment might look like without tutor time altogether.

With its holistic approach, this section aims to equip you with the tools to make informed decisions about tutor time, ensuring it is not only functional but also impactful in meeting the needs of your pupils and school community and your wider school commitments.

Part II Designing a tutor time curriculum

This section provides detailed guidance on designing a tutor time curriculum that aligns with your school's long-term aims and improvement plan. It includes practical advice on structuring your curriculum, using this book as a tool to support the process, and ensuring school-wide success while doing so.

Additionally, this section considers how to use tutor time to ensure that its impact extends beyond daily routines. It offers strategies for building a curriculum that is personalised, suitable and fit for purpose, while also providing practical steps to ensure it can be effectively quality assured, refined and improved upon.

Part III Tutor time for supporting school culture and community

This part considers how tutor time can be used to help induct pupils into the school culture, support school transitions, new school initiatives, establish and support relationships between peers, pupils and staff and share behaviour norms and routines. It also considers the steps we can take during tutor time to build a sense of community and ensure pupils have the best opportunity to build a sense of belonging. It offers guidance and activities for forging and sustaining connections to our immediate and wider communities through annual celebration and commemoration events that can be built into tutor time planning. World Mental Health Day, Anti-Bullying Week and many more important events are discussed with activities and tips suggested.

Part IV Tutor time for health and wellbeing
This part of this book has activities and tips for health and wellbeing activities during tutor time. In this section we will consider the activities which can be done in tutor time to support pupils to feel well and be well, including strategies to help with stress and sleep, providing relevant, realistic and useful information to enable students to develop effective self-care behaviours, understanding and habits.

Part V Tutor time for academic improvement
In this part of this book we will consider how tutor time can be used to support competencies to support academic improvement. Targeted reading, SEN(D) support, revision planning, habit tutoring, target setting and metacognition are just a few of the activities and tips that will be covered.

These sections are structured to reinforce the three primary objectives of any successful tutor programme. All are suggested as activities and focuses following the first and most crucial part of tutor time, to bolster safeguarding efforts through meticulous record-keeping and maintaining a comprehensive understanding of each pupil under your care. These activities have been designed to facilitate the positive relationships and rapport among students and staff, which underpins a sense of community and support. And last, to explore the various ways in which tutor time can be leveraged to promote positive pupil outcomes.

This book aims to be a treasure trove for every teacher who has ever found themselves in charge of a Tutor class! It aims to address these challenges in a way that recognises myriad demands on a teacher's time and the limited capacity for additional tasks. Inside you'll find a wealth of activities that require little to no planning but will have a positive and engaging impact upon your pupils. Schools are like whirlwinds, with teachers spinning multiple plates. Bursting with creativity, tips and activities, this book is your trusty companion, helping you navigate through it all. It is all about making tutor time count, making it meaningful and giving your students (and you) the best start to the day, without gobbling up too much of your precious time.

Part I
Logistics of tutor time

Approaches to tutor time

In my previous book, *A Practical Guide to Pupil Wellbeing*, I discussed the experience I have had teaching in different schools and reflected on my perception that schools are like different countries, where language, cultures and values are varied. Just as pupils are exposed to the 'hidden curriculum', that is, the unspoken or implicit lessons, values and behaviours that are transmitted to pupils through the culture and structure of the educational system, as well as through interactions with teachers, peers, and the environment.

These hidden lessons may include aspects such as social norms, cultural expectations, power dynamics; ways of thinking and behaving that are not explicitly taught but are learned through observation and experience within the educational setting. You as a teacher also come to build up a vast 'community knowledge' of *your* school and how *you* do things *there*. This will be unique to each school you work in. Tutor time is a good example of how a task can be carried out in a myriad ways through different approaches. There are many different ways to approach tutor time, and how it is done in one school is unlikely to be identical to another.

In writing this book I researched hundreds of schools to ascertain how tutor time approaches vary between different schools. It is clearly a common feature in almost every school: just as schools are like different countries, tutor time approaches greatly vary! Tutor time approaches across the land do appear to be designed to enable important duties to be carried out and meaningful relationships to be built. If anything, the research I undertook suggests that what teachers desperately want is not necessarily continuity between schools but more training so they are better placed to meet the needs of their pupils.

It is worthwhile considering how your school approaches its quality assurance for tutor time. Is the pupil voice consulted to ensure their thoughts and needs are considered in the planning? Do other school professionals get an opportunity to reflect on the wider aims of tutor time and contribute? How does your school plan this time to support whole school improvement? Questionnaires at regular intervals can support everyone to ensure that tutor time is effective for the aims of the whole school community and the burden of planning does not rest solely on the individuals delivering it, so this book has been written to alleviate some of that burden.

Time allocations

In researching this book it was important to explore all approaches taken to tutor time so I could ensure this book would be a useful resource to all tutor teachers, regardless of their school's systems. Earlier in the introduction I touched on the variety of names given to this task and discussed the sheer volume of diversity. The majority of schools had some differences in the time allocated to this duty, And not only that but the actual requirements of teachers varied between administrative duties only and more pastoral roles. For example, in one school, tutor time lasted just 10 minutes and was purely undertaken on the basis of having the same, consistent, adult completing the daily register, welcoming pupils in for the day, processing absences, reviewing attendance records – any anomalies or concerns were to be passed to a middle manager.

Another school allocated 25 minutes a day to tutor teachers to undertake administrative duties and deliver the Personal Social Education Curriculum. The approaches of the majority varied in time allocation mostly.

Thousands of teachers responded to the Teacher Tapp question, with the majority indicating that their allocation for tutor time was 15 minutes or more. A small minority had less time than this. The timing allocation is rarely influenced solely by design, but it is often dictated by period length and teaching requirements for the subjects, lunch length and break times. Tutor time approaches are interdependent on the wider school set-up and are interconnected to the wider education approach.

The activities that follow have been mindful of the timeframes teachers have available and can be adapted to suit.

Record Keeping

Of the more than 4,500 teacher responses on Teacher Tapp (2023), over 60% stated that tutor time takes place first thing in the morning. This makes sense as the first duties are often that of register taker – noting down the pupils who are present at the start of the day, and importantly noting those who are not. Absences from school continue to be a national concern. Assessing attendance records is first line safeguarding; many local authorities advocate for an 85%+ attendance rate, after which it becomes a serious safeguarding issue. And you do not have to look far to find official statistics outlining the significant number of young people who are absent from education.

A strong relationship with a tutor can often be the first step in helping pupils who are struggling with school attendance to begin coming back. This might involve one-to-one meetings or organising smaller tutor group sessions – flexibility is essential in making this work effectively.

The role of the tutor, as described, encompasses several crucial responsibilities. First, they are tasked with diligently recording student attendance on a daily basis. This duty is essential for maintaining accurate attendance records. Once attendance is recorded, tutors are responsible for inputting this data into the school's preferred data system. This ensures that attendance records are properly documented, securely stored and accessible to relevant staff. The data collected during tutor time is crucial as it enables issues to be identified and interventions deployed. It is emphasised that thorough training on the registration process is essential for tutors. Changing technology is a double-edged sword for schools and teachers, it often offers more insightful data to be collected, yet change can be burdensome. Understanding the intricacies of the registration process enables everyone in a school to handle attendance data securely, process it accurately and ensure that it can be effectively shared with others who need it.

In addition to attendance monitoring and data entry, tutors undertake various other duties aimed at supporting the smooth functioning of the classroom and promoting pupil readiness for learning and the day ahead. These tasks may include overseeing equipment checks to ensure that necessary classroom materials and resources are available and in good condition, uniform checks and setting intentions for the day ahead.

Attendance

It is highly likely that your school has a software programme that keeps track of school attendance for individuals as well as collating trends across year groups. These platforms have programmes and processing capacity to flag up concerning attendance rates and will gather valuable data to help the wider school safeguarding team monitor pupils. This system is where the registration data you collect will be processed and stored. Along with the safeguarding team it would be helpful for you to have access to assess the trends and norms for your school, so you are armed with the information and supported to be proactive in supporting attendance. We have already discussed the cut-offs and figures that should prompt follow-up and actions so it is worthwhile having a section here to consider the proactive approaches we can take to support attendance and buy-in to tutor time.

Like all people, pupils are much more likely to attend and buy into something when they feel it is worthwhile, and that they are welcome and their social needs are met. In terms of motivation, Self-Determination Theory (SDT), developed by psychologists Richard Ryan and Edward Deci, suggests that three essential psychological needs must be fulfilled for individuals to feel motivated. These needs comprise autonomy, that is the desire to feel in control of one's own life and choices; competence, the need to feel capable and effective in one's actions and achievements; and relatedness, which is the desire to feel connected to others and experience a sense of belonging. When these needs are met, individuals are more likely to be self-motivated and engaged in activities that interest them, bringing them joy and satisfaction. Conversely, if one or more of these needs are absent, pupils may experience negative emotions and engage in unproductive behaviours.

Amy Edmondson's work on psychological safety, although designed with workplace teams in mind, can be a reminder to us in education of the importance that a welcoming, safe and supportive 'team' environment can have for enabling us to get the best out of our pupils. Psychological safety, as Edmondson defines it, is a shared belief among team members that they can express ideas, ask questions, raise concerns and make mistakes without fear of embarrassment, punishment or retaliation. Her research highlights that when individuals feel psychologically safe, they are more likely to take risks that lead to growth, development and improvement within the organisation. Edmondson's work proposes that psychologically safe teams and environments including hospitals are more likely to report errors and mistakes than workplaces which lack the necessary supportive environments. In schools, we can do our best to enable pupils to bridge the gap between their home life and school through welcoming, routine tutor sessions that help ease pupils into their day. This is one small way tutors can contribute to reducing the trend of school residuals and absence.

Within your school, you can use the SDT theory and Amy Edmondson's work to inform your tutor time curriculum planning. By focusing on the three key psychological needs outlined in the theory, autonomy, competence and relatedness, we can design a tutor time curriculum that encourages active participation, personal growth and supports pupils striving for their next steps challenging themselves.

In order to promote and support autonomy to provide pupils with choices, throughout this book there are different strategies and methods suggested for various things. Integrating elements of choice within these activities is one effective and accessible strategy to support the need for autonomy in the curriculum.

The information on these pages has been carefully designed to support excellent school outcomes. Designing a tutor time curriculum that provides pupils with the opportunity to enhance their skills, knowledge and awareness is an important step to making sure tutor time is important, useful and workable to them and therefore encourages healthy attendance.

And last, to support the need for relatedness, these activities and ideas have been carefully planned to facilitate a sense of community within the tutor group. When pupils feel they belong and are valued within the learning environment, and their emotional and social needs are met, this further enhances wellbeing and positive outcomes.

The planning and delivery of an excellent tutor time curriculum is a proactive step in supporting good attendance, raising pupil confidence and coping strategies for academic, personal and social life. Sharing the terms' plan and inviting pupils to contribute to it and selecting the sessions they feel would be beneficial is a strategy to support buy-in from pupils too. Effective monitoring and tracking through registration and administrative duties is a vital step to help respond and work through attendance issues that occur. It enables tutor teachers the opportunity to connect and communicate with and support all pupils in fundamental but vital ways.

Organisation/SEND

Tutors also play a role in helping students organise their academic responsibilities by setting up and maintaining homework diaries or planners.

This assists students in managing their assignments and deadlines effectively, promoting good study habits and organisational skills. At different times during the year this support might become more important. For example, when pupils have deadlines for coursework, tutor teachers can help pupils stay organised and prioritise their workload accordingly. More on this on page 71–74.

This is especially helpful for neurodivergent pupils for whom the daily requirements, organisation and changing stimulus can present additional challenges. The nature of school, the environment, expectations and stimulus can be overwhelming for pupils and especially neurodivergent pupils. Statistics indicate that a frightening majority of young people with school avoidance issues fall into the neurodivergent umbrella: 92.1% of children experiencing school attendance difficulties are neurodivergent, with 83.5% being autistic (according to a sample by Connolly and Mullally, 2022). Additionally, children with Special Educational Needs are 50% more likely to struggle with school attendance (Office for National Statistics, 2021). Furthermore, 31% of autistic children and young people are persistently absent from school (Ambitious about Autism, 2022).

Meanwhile, the existing SEND system continues to be strained by ongoing budget constraints, time limitations and shortages of teachers. The repercussions of an inadequately supported education system can be extrapolated from the data from PISA and the Good Childhood report which suggests lower life satisfaction, lower attendance and happiness rates among young people with SEND. While the solutions to this crisis of SEND provision may not be solved overnight, creating inclusive schools should not be a summit to conquer but an ongoing endeavour which requires trust, time and commitment. Schools can take steps towards becoming more inclusive by creating a valuable, purposeful approach to tutor time. Designing consistent, calm, predictable learning environments which feature routine is key to creating certainty that can help ameliorate the stresses and worries of pupils who, when presented with unfamiliarity, can struggle. Creating an additional opportunity to support all pupils is worthwhile and, for some, essential.

Tutors have an opportunity to engage in activities and share information or routines that help students transition into the school day. This may involve sharing of information reiterating expectations, discussions or other interactions aimed at preparing students mentally and emotionally for the day ahead. Creating these catch-all approaches is not a solution to the SEND crisis, but is an example of how we can build capacity into the existing system to promote inclusive environments that support all learners.

Overall, the role of the tutor is diverse, encompassing administrative responsibilities such as attendance monitoring and data entry, as well as providing support and guidance to students to enhance their educational experience. It is a role that is likely to vary depending upon your school. Just as in any industry, the first point of contact is critical, be in customer service or in a busy private business, and so is the first port of contact in schools. Your role as a tutor teacher can be the optimal/pivotal opportunity to deeply support, encourage and include all children where consistent, relevant and useful interaction and discussion can engage the students in a positive and relatively safe environment, away from attainment and achievement.

But it's not just the organisation of pupils that needs to be considered, a need to build greater capacity into school timetables and maximise efficiencies means that more and more teachers may find themselves responsible for tutor time above and beyond their timetable commitments; this is especially within academy schools, and within the independent sector. With huge demands on their time, being a tutor can be an unwanted gift that eats into already busy schedules.

Schools without tutor time

I spoke to hundreds of schools in the process of research for this book and a small minority who had removed tutor time from their timetables. I spoke directly to three secondary schools who had opted to permanently dissolve this feature of their school day. All three, separately, told us that this had been driven by financial constraints and eliminating the requirement for teachers to undertake tutor time had resulted in them having greater capacity for timetabled teaching periods. The drivers for changing the school day were unsurprising to hear: these schools were hard pressed to build greater capacity to deliver the curriculum and had to use creative ways of doing so. What was surprising however was the level of disruptions and difficulty in making the decision to dissolve tutor time.

The first of the three schools we spoke to has since reversed their decision, and is reinstating tutor time from the next academic year, stating that only in its absence had they been forced to identify its importance for pupil wellbeing, staff and school systems. Information sharing had been a particular challenge and many notices and important updates had been difficult to communicate. One teacher noted that the information shared in tutor time not only benefited the pupils, but also enabled him to have a full overview of events and activities taking place. Without tutor time he said he felt his community knowledge suffered and that had a knock-on effect to his understanding of the kids. For example, it was standard practice for sporting fixtures to be announced via tutor time tutors, and not having to do this meant this teacher was less able to organise their planning around important events which may have resulted in pupils being absent from their class. they commented that it made them less able to highlight positive outcomes and pupil successes as there was neither the time nor information available. Sharing information with staff as well as pupils is not a key driver for tutor time, but it was an interesting, and significant, casualty when this school abandoned it. It is a worthy point to consider; our ability to fully support our young people requires knowledge of them and their experiences outside of our classroom, and gaining this information in tutor time seems a happy by-product of the time invested.

As school days comprise non-stop engagement, with just about every minute timetabled for specific use, it was unsurprising that shuffling notices and updates into the first learning period of the day posed some problems, an issue highlighted by these schools. Classroom teachers responsible for the first period of the were quick to stress the negative impact on the flow and delivery of their curriculum content in starting their lessons with notices and tutor time activities. Lessons were less focused after teachers had spent upwards of ten minutes reading through upcoming plans, school news and various reminders. Without the distinct break between this activity and the first lesson beginning, teachers felt their pupils were harder to re-engage with and the learning routine suffered. A second point here was that teachers felt there was a disproportionate impact on their curriculum coverage when the same subject was hit multiple times in the week with tutor time duties.

Another finding was that removing tutor time had inadvertently placed an undue burden on the schools' guidance system. Without designated 'frontline guidance support' guidance teachers and pastoral leads had a greater requirement to undertake administrative duties which compromised their ability to support their own caseloads. Additional duties included the guidance teacher having the new responsibility to monitor and chase late arrivals, monitor absence, check uniform and also equipment infractions. This had resulted in the poor use of middle managers who spent time chasing information and were less able to respond to the wellbeing needs and more serious issues of others until the administrative roles were complete. It also created wider cracks for pupils to fall through and made the safeguarding duty harder to implement and manage effectively.

Typically, one of the central roles of a tutor teacher is to monitor and flag up young people with school avoidance issues. An unaccounted-for attendance rate of less than 85% is deemed a potential safeguarding matter that requires interventions and follow-up. With a robust system for tutor time, early interventions can ensure issues are managed before rates of absences creep to such a high number. With record numbers of school refusals and the vital need for early intervention, not having a designated person to oversee daily patterns makes this job much harder to carry out.

The second of the three schools was smaller and more able to apply flexibility to their decision. In place of daily tutor time, they introduced group morning meetings instead. This had come after a trial when period 1 teachers had been responsible for registering pupil attendance and sharing notes. Again, the time disruptions caused to staff and the impact this had on curriculum delivery prompted Senior Leaders to consider an alternative solution that still freed up teaching capacity. And so their day started with mixed-year-group assemblies. There were accommodation challenges as well as content challenges and a reluctant admission that the quality of *real assemblies* had suffered.

Environment

It is worth noting the impact that room allocation and environmental stimulus can have on behaviour. In schools where tutor sessions are delivered to whole year groups, the accommodation needs require careful consideration. I spoke to a school where the gym hall and canteen were frequently used for these activities. The behavioural prompts and associations within these settings are notably different to the ones in classrooms. All human behaviour is impacted by environmental stimuli: take, for example, the way we instinctively behave in a church or mosque, we are quiet, respectful, slow and purposeful in our movements. This is very different to how we behave at a football match, where often joyful, loud and outgoing behaviours can be seen.

The volume of demands on a pupil in school is huge. From the behavioural prompts, to the explicit instructions to shape behaviour, to the unwritten rules of behaviour seldom mentioned but observed, copied and normalised, pupils have a lot to consider. But often in schools the almost somewhat 'innate' unuttered rules which are not always explicit and lack written instructions dictating the behavioural responses can create a breakdown in communication and therefore prevent and hinder our pupils from learning the expectations and therefore meeting them.

Within the classroom it can be easier to control the prompts and ensure that behaviour is guided and shaped with feedback – written and unwritten, spoken and unspoken – given to help modify and direct it towards the desired outcomes and norms to further establish and reinforce them. Whereas within areas which are typically more social spaces or in sports halls where a different type of behaviour and action is expected and required, it can add another layer of challenges in making these spaces multifunctional. Later, on page 64, I will discuss the use of tutor time for practising behaviour routines and exploring the desired outcomes with pupils too.

Field theory

Psychological theorists offer insightful ideas as to why human behaviour is sensitive to our environment: notably, Kurt Lewin, a pioneering German-American psychologist known for his work in social psychology, and particularly his development of *field theory*. Lewin worked on field theory (1942), evidencing that human behaviour is directly influenced by the 'field' or environmental stimulus we are exposed to at any given time. According to his theory, behaviour is the result of the interaction between a person's psychological state and the situational forces present in different settings. For example, a pupil who is fairly motivated in school will apply themselves in an appropriate manner within a library or study room environment. However, a pupil who is equally motivated may struggle to study in a similarly quiet coffee shop as the behavioural prompts lead to different expected behaviours.

So it is not surprising that using canteens and other multipurpose settings can lead to additional challenges to setting expectations and norms. If possible, carefully consider the environment in which you deliver this all-important start to the day. Ideally, opting for somewhere that pupils have a clear sense of the consistent expected behaviour optimises appropriate interactions, behaviours and expectation.

However, as I write this book, I am acutely aware that some schools won't have the luxury of any options and even if you do, it will be time well spent in considering how to support pupils learn the expectations of tutor time. Consider: are there any steps you can take to set the space up differently to support a more focused environment as opposed to social? How do you communicate the different expectations to pupils? We can't hold pupils wholly responsible for not upholding expectations if they are not clearly taught, explained and supported to follow. More on supporting pupils with this on page 68.

Sensory load

Within the chosen space or environment it is important to pay some attention to the room itself and consider, along the behaviour prompts the space holds, how does it feel to be in that space? Busy, loud, colourful, bold classrooms can seem pretty and vibrant but we also need to review the flip side of this. Our capacity to process the cognitive load we are exposed to plays a huge role in behaviour, conduct and feelings within our environment and while no one expects teachers and school staff to be experts in human psychology, there are a few key points to note and apply here. In part, how a young person feels (and learns, more on this on page 132) is influenced by the sensory load of their setting.

The human processing ability is not infinite and we can only hold so much in our short-term attention. Considering how this impacts a pupil's behaviour and learning is essential in order to ensure we are giving them the best chance of success. The brain's ability to process, respond to and cope is affected by the noises, smells, lights and design of the environment we are in.

This sensory load has a direct impact on cognition, and therefore learning. Think about the annoying ticking of a clock in a quiet room, or the buzzing of a fly trapped at a closed window. The forces hold our attention and can start to build feelings (perhaps not positive ones) for us. Compare that to the quiet focus you have when your desk is clear and the environment you are in enables you to choose your focus.

Some pupils may struggle more with managing their sensory load than others as their executive function will be at different stages of development, but this can be an easy win for teachers. Within education, consider the automatic doors – that is, the actions which are helpful for all, like automatic doors in the supermarket, but essential for some, for example those with mobility issues. Designing the learning environment with this in mind is an easy win. I wholly believe that there are few classroom rooms which cannot be improved by removing at least three things! In considering the space for tutor time, it is crucial to remember how the environment creates behavioural prompts.

It is vital to consider that pupils are unique individuals and while we may not have a huge impact on their psychological state on any given day, we can help them by first teaching and establishing expected behaviour in different school settings, and also by ensuring appropriate behaviour prompts support the establishment of these becoming norms. Thoughtful room design, daylight and fresh air are vital to ensure our pupils have the best chance to direct their focus and attention on the things we want them to.

Alternatives to tutor time

The school mentioned above was keen to acknowledge that moving to a large group delivery for tutor time was the least bad option they could come up with. It was one that enabled money to be saved, capacity created and the essential role of tutor time to be supported as best it could. Schools and school leaders are forced more and more to be creative in their ability to create capacity and meet the needs of many. Whatever choices your school has had to make, it is important to consider the ways you can work within those constraints to support young people and yourself to make the most of tutor time.

And the third school I spoke with said they were sticking to their decision to abolish tutor time purely due to ongoing financial constraints. They discussed similar difficulties to the ones discussed above but said their need to build greater capacity into the teaching loads meant that sacrificing tutor time was, regrettably, the casualty of choice.

As part of wider educational interventions, a couple of other schools had changed the content of tutor time and used it almost entirely to facilitate literacy/numeracy interventions with pupils. We will discuss this approach on page 136.

Whatever the approach to tutor time, my research underpins what I suspected to be true. Far from being an add-on, tutor time provides an explicit opportunity to enhance the experience and success of our pupils. It is a worthy entry in our busy school day and one I hope this book assists you with.

In 1911, Leonardo Di Vinci's lesser-known painting at the time, the 'Mona Lisa', was stolen from her place in the Louvre. In the days that followed a nation in shock swarmed to witness the blank space in which she had previously been displayed. Prior to the theft, the 'Mona Lisa' was admired mainly by art critics and scholars for Leonardo da Vinci's masterful technique and the mystery behind the subject's smile. She was not a household name or as universally recognised as the painting is now. When the painting was stolen, the story became a sensational news event, covered extensively in international media. And over the next two years, until she was returned, more people visited this empty spot where she had hung than had come to see her in the preceding months. This widespread coverage brought the 'Mona Lisa' to the attention of the general public, making it a cultural phenomenon.

The drama surrounding its disappearance, the mystery of how it was stolen and its eventual recovery in 1913 turned the 'Mona Lisa' into one of the most famous works of art in the world.

She was more powerful and important in her absence than she had been when she was present. And through missing her, she was propelled to worldwide fame and valued more greatly than she had been before. It seems that we are often better placed to miss something once there is something there to miss, we take for granted what has always been and can fail to recognise the significance of something until we are left experiencing the impact of its loss. In behavioural economics this is known as endowment bias whereby people place higher values on things they already own rather than things they do not. For the 'Mona Lisa', the public or cultural ownership of the painting may have triggered a similar emotional reaction whereby people felt its loss more acutely once it was gone, leading to an increased sense of its value.

This anecdote of the 'Mona Lisa' certainly resonated with the three schools we spoke to who, by their own admission, felt that this 'anchor' in the day represented an opportunity to build positive relationships, prepare for the day ahead and provide autonomy for teachers to direct the time as they felt appropriate, and missed it once it was gone.

Of the hundreds of schools I did speak to, some common themes did emerge. There was a desire to have the continuity of the tutor teacher throughout the year and where possible for the tutor teacher to remain with the class throughout their time in school. It was deemed that this enabled positive relationships to be built over the years that a pupil was in school and also well placed the teacher to identify issues or needs for support. Cornelius-White's (2007) meta-analysis reveals that significant impacts on student attainment result from strong, positive teacher-pupil relationships in the classroom. Additionally, these positive relationships act as protective factors against pressing issues such as poor behaviour, absenteeism and the decision to leave schooling. The work of Roorda et al. (2011) demonstrated a similar strong connection between positive teacher-pupil relationships and student achievement. Hattie (2009) references both of these studies to bolster his argument, suggesting that when teachers prioritise building robust relationships with their students early in the academic year, and the outcomes include increased engagement, greater self and mutual respect, reduced resistance, more student-initiated activities and improved learning results (p. 119). This is not limited to the teacher delivering the academic lessons but extends to tutor teachers and support staff.

In discussion, one of the most universally valued aspects of tutor time is consistency of the tutor. Staff, pupils and parents alike voice an appreciation of being able to stick with the same set-up over multiple years.

One of my close friends, Emma, works as a medic. I recall a conversation between us years ago when she shared the news of her sister's pregnancy with me, brimming with excitement. When I inquired about how her sister shared this happy news with her, Emma gently corrected me, revealing that her sister hadn't directly informed her. Clearly my face gave away my surprise and puzzlement at these revelations before asking Emma to explain exactly how she knew!

Emma, drawing from her extensive experience, confided that she simply had a knack for sensing pregnancy in others. She attributed it to a mix of finely tuned observation skills, a touch of intuition, deep knowledge of her sister and her medical expertise, recognising the subtle signs of early pregnancy that often go unnoticed. I will be as honest here as I was with her, she sounded convincing but left me feeling less than convinced that she possessed such skills. Yet, sure enough, a few weeks later, Emma's sister made the official announcement, and Emma embraced the news with surprise and joy, as any supportive sibling would.

This experience has often stayed in my thoughts. As I make sense of it, I see that much like Emma, teachers often possess an innate sense of when a student requires assistance, guidance or encouragement. We are often able to sense that 'something' isn't quite right even though we may not be able to articulate our reasoning. Through years of exposure to similar situations, we develop an intuitive understanding of those under our care, attuned to their nonverbal cues and body language. We may not always know the source of the issue, but more often than not, when we suspect there is an issue, we are right. And it is vital that we have the professional support and trust to voice any such concerns. Having consistent, daily contact with one group of pupils enables us to build a fuller understanding of who they are, what they need and how we can use the school system to support them. It might not be the role you originally applied for, or even want, but it is a crucial position that carries significant importance and positive influence.

Setting up tutor time

If you are a teacher reading this book for hints and tips to support your tutor session, it is unlikely that you will have had much input into the time allocation, expectations or systems used to allocate pupils into tutor groupings. It will, however, be your job to make the best out of whichever route your leadership team have steered the ship into. There are likely to be a number of factors the leadership team did take into consideration when decisions were made about how to structure tutor classes. Or perhaps the current leadership team inherited a structure already in place. If that is the case then it is worth considering the various methods of structuring tutor time below.

If you are in a position to do so, it is worth undertaking a review for tutor time across your school. Undertaking an audit of the current processes across the year groups might feel unnecessary and intrusive, however through thoughtful collaboration and design, tutor time is a powerful opportunity to not only enhance provision, but also establish powerful routines and habits which create an excellent school environment for everyone.

Author and former school leader, Mary Myatt's book *Back on Track* suggests our workload can be streamlined if we examine our actions in schools and ensure they align with our education aims and objectives. Tutor time is a great example of this, this crucial time can be used for so many positive activities and actions to underpin our wider school aims and ambitions. For example, in a school which identifies behaviour issues, designing activities, messages and reflection/discussion time to teach an accessible and actionable behaviour curriculum is an effective way of supporting both pupil attainment and teacher wellbeing. In a turnaround school where there are identified targets to improve literacy, creating a guided programme with the morning tutor time can again help support these aims and ambitions without creating additional time and teachers. Ensuring your actions in tutor time align with the wider aims of your school is a seamless way of enhancing the experiences of everyone in your school community.

There are a number of different approaches to organising tutor classes. I spoke to hundreds of schools and one of the questions I posed was just that:

how does your school allocate pupils into tutors? The majority of responses linked their aims to their approaches. Many cited that, post-pandemic, the need to ensure socialisation and social cohesion had emerged greater than ever. This pressing need has significantly influenced the design of tutor groups, which my findings showed were crafted to ensure that students share commonalities with their peers.

Primarily, age, year groups and house systems emerged as the most prevalent criteria utilised for organising tutor groups. Pupils were typically set into single-year subgroups depending upon the school's established house system – think of how significant it was for Harry Potter. Hogwarts is divided into four houses, each bearing the last name of its founder: Godric Gryffindor, Salazar Slytherin, Rowena Ravenclaw and Helga Hufflepuff. For the young protagonist this allocation was more than just a means to organise groups of pupils, the house he was sorted into was deeply connected to this identity.

And while we aren't living in the mythical land of wizards and muggles, school house systems are traditional organisational structures found in most schools across the land. They're practical and make good sense to establish a manageable way of organising pupils into groups within school. Pupils are divided into smaller groups or houses, this serves as both an admin purpose and, hopefully, a social one. These smaller groups might be year-group specific as is most common; or in smaller schools I spoke to the house system was used to create vertical integration of year groups, and each group had pupils from that house, of different ages.

Through the house system, pupils can build connections, and gain leadership experience and a sense of belonging to a group extending beyond their immediate peers. Typically, pupils are assigned to a specific house upon starting at the school; this can be done through discussion with primary schools, consideration of older sibling and family connections or at random.

Often, schools name each house after notable figures, areas of local interest, historical importance, colours or other distinguishing features. Each house will incorporate pupils from across all year groups within the school and encourage vertical integration through activities, competitions and events. And just as it was for Harry Potter, this, hopefully, helps share a pupil's connection with their school and tutors as part of the social identity. In Walton et al.'s 2012 work, 'Mere belonging: The power of social connections', their research highlights that a just sense of connectedness enhances achievement motivation.

If your school has a vertical tutor group system in place, which incorporates pupils from different year groups, it is essential to consider the unique dynamics that this arrangement presents when setting up tutor time. In these mixed age groups, pupils who are less familiar with each other may find it challenging to engage in the conversations and interactions that typically occur among peers with more shared experiences such as classes and stages. This lack of familiarity can sometimes lead to hesitancy in initiating discussions or participating in group activities as openly as pupils may do with peers in the same year as them.

To support pupils with this, it is highly advisable to provide structured chat activities that encourage dialogue and interaction. Focusing on existing commonalities such as a shared school house, common interests or extracurricular activities can help break the ice and create a more inclusive environment. Consider incorporating icebreaker games or discussion prompts that highlight these shared connections. This approach not only facilitates communication but also fosters a sense of belonging and community among the pupils.

In a vertical tutor group, the tutor will need to consider their approaches to each activity carefully to ensure that they are pitched at an appropriate level to support and challenge everyone in the room, regardless of age. This attention to detail will help engage all pupils and make each session meaningful. In an ideal world, over time and with support, a vertical tutor group system can lead to a more connected school community as pupils become more familiar with one another and engage in structured activities. This process not only enhances relationships among pupils but also contributes to a more positive atmosphere within the school. With well-established buddy systems in place, older pupils can continue to provide valuable guidance and support to younger pupils.

That said, schools are rarely perfect and the challenges of establishing these relationships should not be underestimated. Building trust and familiarity takes time and consistent effort from both staff and pupils. It is essential to remain patient and committed, understanding that the process may involve setbacks along the way.

Implementing a buddy system within your tutor time can significantly enhance these dynamics. Pairing older pupils who have greater experience within the school with younger pupils allows for mentorship and guidance. This system can be particularly beneficial during transition phases, such as when younger pupils are moving into a New Year group or adapting to different routines. Older pupils can provide insights, share their experiences and help younger pupils navigate the social landscape of the school.

However, it is crucial to provide ongoing support and input to ensure that all pupils feel comfortable and empowered to connect with one another. Regular check-ins and feedback sessions can help identify any challenges that arise and allow for adjustments to be made to the buddy system or group activities. By creating an environment that nurtures relationships and facilitates open communication, you can help all pupils thrive in a vertical tutor group setting.

In many schools the house system provides a valuable opportunity for pupils to gain leadership and mentoring experiences; senior pupils are often captains or prefects, responsible for representing their house, organising house events and providing guidance and support to fellow house members. They play a crucial role in maintaining the spirit and competitiveness of their house. So what starts off as shared experience in tutor time can, with support, permeate through the school system to help solidify the social interactions which are so important for young people and their development. Gökmen Arslan's (2021) study, which encompassed an extensive investigation including interviews with numerous school-aged students, contributes further evidence, demonstrating that inclusion and exclusion experiences within schools indirectly influenced mental health issues through subjective wellbeing. This research underscores the significance of school-based strategies focused on fostering a sense of belonging to address community dynamics and promote wellbeing within the school environment. Until we truly feel a sense of belonging and connection, our school experiences, learning and wellbeing will be compromised.

For example, Inter-house competitions, which will almost certainly take place outside tutor time, are a common feature of the house system. These competitions can span various activities such as sports tournaments, academic quizzes, music and drama performances and charity fundraising events. Participation in these competitions encourages teamwork, sportsmanship and healthy competition among students and they can support positive social transitions for pupils new to the school. It also creates a sense of camaraderie and achievement amongst pupils and staff too, all of which are highly impactful for underpinning effective tutor time.

Organising pupils into house-focused tutor classes makes good sense and enables these events to be organised and pupils to get feedback on how their house is performing. Schools often implement reward systems within the house system to recognise students' achievements and contributions. Points may be awarded for academic excellence, sportsmanship, leadership and participation in house activities.

Using this as a system to set tutor groups also supports the framework for pastoral care and support within the school community. My research showed that guidance staff often had a caseload of pupils who all belonged to the same house and this system enabled guidance teachers to drop in on tutor classes during tutor time to follow-up and check-in.

Overall, the school house system is a step towards building a sense of belonging, identity and therefore community among students. Managed well, it can promote leadership, teamwork and personal development while enhancing school spirit and cohesion but will require regular ongoing support from tutors and house captains.

There were few other systems as popular as using the house system to guide tutor time classes but they do include: specialisation or needs-based approaches. For example, in one school, pupils were reorganised in Year 9 in line with their GCSE choices. Pupils who were studying STEM-based subjects were grouped in classes together where possible and so on. The argument here was that it enabled tutor time to be used to engage with targeted subject support. Equally, a number of schools used tutor time to build capacity into their SEN(D) provision. Pupils with designated needs were in tutor classes together and had daily targeted support. Though it is important not to create grouping, pupils perceive it to be on ability basis. The social interactions which take place during Form Time are a key part of any successful tutor Curriculum and must not be eroded for the sole aim of creating more time for academic activities. There is more on page 142 about how tutor time can support inclusive practices.

Whatever the system used to design this area of school life, it is worth ensuring that it is consistent. Ideally, a teacher being allocated a tutor time for the year, or even better, where feasible for multiple years, helps establish positive familiarity and can support a myriad of social interactions and connections. Consider the physiological phenomenon known as 'mere exposure effect' also known as 'familiarity effect' which suggests that people tend to develop a preference for things they are familiar with. This means that when our pupils have already come across something, they're proven to be more likely to prefer it to an unknown alternative.

For example, in tutor time, socialising with the same group peers each morning becomes preferable and they might end up liking the group more because it feels familiar, even if they hadn't previously gravitated towards this grouping. This effect doesn't just impact our choices about people and groups – it applies to activities, food, words, art and even subjects. There are two main reasons why this happens: it certainly helps to reduce feelings of uncertainty and it is easier for your brain to process things that it is already familiar with and decision making in these conditions is less of a burden on cognitive functions.

In school we can exploit this phenomenon and ensure that through familiarity with tutor social groups we can ensure they feel more comfortable and at ease in their presence. This familiarity can alleviate feelings of shyness or stress that might otherwise inhibit their participation in activities; later we will discuss the importance of tutor time for effective transition. These positive feelings of familiarity pay even when pupils may feel more confident in participating in house activities when they see their friends or familiar faces engaging in the activity. This sense of social validation can reinforce their willingness to join in.

Pupils who already know each other have likely established social connections and rapport. This can create a sense of belonging and camaraderie, making it more appealing for students to participate in activities together as they feel supported and accepted within the group. Consistent tutor groups also enable the teacher to identify pupils who may need a little more support with socialising – see page 53 for more details on this.

Last, previous positive interactions with peers can create positive associations with group activities – especially unfamiliar ones. Our pupils may associate the activity with enjoyable experiences they've had with their peers in the past, further motivating them to join in, doing it as a group creates less self-exposure and can be comforting.

Overall, the exposure effect highlights the importance of familiarity in influencing behaviour. This phenomenon underscores the role of social connections and comfort in facilitating participation and engagement and adds a body of weight to the argument for creating tutor classes based on common school themes.

Part II
Designing a tutor time curriculum

Tutor time is an opportunity to create and sustain improvements on both a micro and macro level. In terms of supporting whole-school initiatives, tutor time enables notices, updates and information to be shared more intimately than in assemblies. This can be hugely effective for establishing behaviour norms and creates an opportunity for pupils to ask questions, gain assistance and seek clarity in a way that is hindered in traditionally assemblies. In a time when headlines are frequently adorned with damning reports on behaviour, attendance and attainment, these sessions can be tailored to support the school improvement aims and plans.

On an individual level, tutor time greatly helps with administrative tasks, the school house system and can even offer a system to help ensure everyone has their protractor for the day, but let's not overlook the powerful force it can have for improvement.

Over the last few years there has been an explosion of books being published to help everyday readers make and sustain better habits: for example *Atomic Habits* by James Clear, *The Power of Habit* by Charles Duhigg, *Tiny Habits* by B.J. Fogg and many more popular books offer wisdom, research and advice for setting positive behaviour patterns and improving behaviours. James Clear notes the significant impact Dave Brailsford had when he joined the underperforming British Cycling team as General Manager and Performance Director for Team Sky.

Knowing that British cyclists had won just one gold medal since 1908, David took a different approach to improvement, the 1% rule. Rather than chasing overnight success, he focused on making small, marginal gains in every possible area. The idea was simple, if they could improve by just 1% in multiple areas, the cumulative impact would be transformational. He supported improvement in a variety of seemingly obscure things: for example, the pillows each team member slept on were changed to ensure maximum rest, and he brought in a surgeon to teach the team how to wash their hands thoroughly to prevent the spread of viruses and bugs. The idea behind aggregation of marginal gains is to make small, incremental improvements in multiple areas, with the belief that the cumulative effect of these small, maintainable improvements will lead to significant overall improvement.

Instead of focusing solely on making one big improvement – which can often be insurmountable, such as investing in expensive equipment or drastically overhauling the curriculum – the approach of aggregation of marginal gains involves identifying and improving numerous small factors that collectively contribute to success. For us, this could include factors like uniform, attendance, engagement in co-curricular activities and study habits and the micro habits which form a bigger picture of who the learner is and how they approach their work.

By paying attention to and optimising each of these small factors, the theory suggests that the overall outcomes will improve incrementally. Even though each individual improvement may seem minor on its own, when aggregated together, over time, they can result in a substantial overall enhancement.

Although first applied to the sporting world, Brailsford implemented this approach to the British Cycling team with great success and it is a concept that can easily be applied to a host of industries and activities. The concept of aggregation of marginal gains can be applied beyond sports and is relevant in various fields where performance improvement is desired, including within education, and through tutor time we can manage and support the attainment of these small gains. This theory shows the importance of continuous improvement and the cumulative impact of making small, incremental changes over time. This concept aligns perfectly with the gradual process of improvement inherent in schools and second nature to teachers.

Like Dave Brailsford, teachers instinctively (and often unconsciously) analyse and refine their practice, knowing that real progress comes from consistent, incremental improvement rather than instant results. This gradual, step-by-step approach is at the heart of what we do, teaching is, after all, the process of breaking down complex ideas into manageable steps and improving them over time.

It is both practical and wise to focus on improving micro-actions, behaviours, and strategies rather than imposing sweeping, overnight reforms, both from the perspective of impact and teacher wellbeing. Take vocabulary development, for example. Whether in a pupil's first language or an additional one, we do not expect them to memorise the entire dictionary at once. Instead, we build their knowledge through repeated exposure and retrieval, hearing, reading, writing and using new words in context until, over time, they develop fluency.

The same principle applies to tutor time. By focusing on key areas (academic, social and wellbeing), we can take a structured, piecemeal approach that, over time, strengthens pupils' knowledge, skills and confidence. Small, deliberate steps lead to lasting transformation that is sustainable and appropriate for all teaching staff to engage with, despite their busy workloads.

In case you need more convincing of this approach, in just five years after Dave Brailsford took over, the British Cycling team rose from failure to dominate both road and track cycling at the 2008 Beijing Olympic Games, winning an incredible eight gold medals. Four years later, at the London Olympics they achieved success again and set nine Olympic and seven world records.

In that same year, Bradley Wiggins became the first British cyclist to win the Tour de France, and the following year, his teammate Chris Froome claimed victory, before doing so again in 2015, 2016 and 2017.

Between 2007 and 2017, British cyclists won 178 world championships, 66 Olympic or Paralympic gold medals, and claimed five Tour de France victories, an era now regarded as one of the most successful in cycling history, all down to 1% in improvements. And I believe that through a well-thought-out, planned tutor time curriculum we can replicate this impressive run (less the world records!).

School improvement planning

Through careful planning and effectively designing a tutor time curriculum, this book can help schools gain up to 45 hours (based on the nominal 15 minutes a day for tutor time) annually to support whole-school improvement goals. What is better, is that with the day-to-day reinforcement of desired outcomes comes a greater chance of success, just as the 1% of marginal gains can build up to a huge impact: daily opportunities to 'habit stack' can create opportunities to nurture whole-school improvement.

A daily 15-minute tutor time session can support habit formation, wellbeing and academic improvement through the principle of habit stacking, a concept where new behaviours are linked to established routines to make them easier to adopt. By attaching small, consistent actions such as reinforcing the important daily social expectations within the school setting, setting goals and encouraging pupils to reflect on their progress, pupils can be supported to form micro habits that reinforce positive behaviour and well-being over time. This regular and manageable approach helps build momentum, as tiny habits accumulate, leading to long-term improvement. The key is consistency: the 'little and often' approach ensures that these micro habits become ingrained in pupils' routines, promoting both personal development and academic success.

The key, therefore, is to ensure your tutor curriculum reflects the goals and aims of your school. This might be harder to do without support from the powers above, however in an ideal scenario the tutor time curriculum will be expertly aligned to your school's values and goals. This can be done on a classroom basis if necessary.

In general terms all schools will have a Whole-School Improvement Plan which is available to all stakeholders. These plans should be aligned to the values and goals of the schools, and as such they will change and evolve year on year. These plans will consider the most concerning issues impacting whole-school features and note the opportunities that exist for improvement within these challenges. Good whole-school improvement plans will be based on existing data, for example through surveying teachers to enquire about the biggest issues they face in terms of teaching and learning, or to consider the data relating to pupil absence, school refusal and mental health. These findings will be synthesised to create actionable next steps which can be measured and implemented within the school. Detailed approaches and logistics should be considered when designing the journey towards each of these targets. It may sound like a daunting task but think of it more as a jigsaw puzzle which, done well, can lead to whole-school improvement for all stakeholders.

Developing a school improvement plan is a dynamic and comprehensive process that should extend beyond simple goal-setting. It requires a rigorous, evidence-informed approach and involves thorough data analysis which enables leaders to set measurable objectives, identify opportunities with complex challenges and create targeted strategies for improvement as well as acknowledging that improvement is seldom quick or easy! School improvement plans are not a quick solution but should be viewed as a tool towards a sustainable journey of improvement. To be effective, they demand commitment, adaptability and a culture of continuous improvement.

Most whole-school improvement plans are written documents that are widely accessible. Many will incorporate the following:

- the school's overarching vision and values;
- pre-existing audit findings;
- contextual details of the school, including factors that support or challenge performance improvement;
- improvement areas identified through self-assessment, Ofsted, HMIE inspections or external evaluations including stakeholders;
- goals set for pupil achievement;
- goals set for improving the quality of teaching;
- specific objectives, improvement actions, success criteria and indicators of good practice for each goal;
- clear timelines for actions with designated leaders for each priority;
- a breakdown of the resources necessary to implement the actions;
- a description of the methods for tracking and assessing the progress of the plan.

Below is an example of an extract of whole-school improvement plan:

Designing a tutor time curriculum

	Aims/Intent	Action/Task	Success Criteria	Personnel	Resource Needs	Timescale	Progress
Teaching and Learning	Increase and further develop reading attainment in Year 7	Evaluate strengths and weaknesses of current approaches Resource development Teach retrieval Revisit phonics where necessary	• Measure ORF aim for improvements across the year group • Assess pupil experiences of reading buddy system • Phonics testing for BAR pupils	DHT Whole-school literacy teachers Librarian SENCO	In-house staff coaching HTYP Resource packs Library budget Digital resources	12 months	Option 1 (e.g. yet to start)
School Culture	Develop effective corridor behaviours	Using explicit instruction, teach a predesigned behaviour curriculum	• Monthly reduction on corridor incidents • Improved supervising staff experiences • Sample pupil experiences across all year groups for evidence of improved experiences	DHT behaviour All school staff to reinforce	Time School Code of Conduct Communication home Assembly times	12 months	Option 2 (e.g. in progress)
Curriculum	Provide greater opportunities for Year 12 pupils to engage in super curricular activities	Assess and evaluate opportunities for external events, competitions and experiences Develop and in-house offering	• Enhanced offered of activities within each curricular area • Sample data to assess	Department heads Respective SLT All staff External where necessary	Staffing Budget for external events SLT support Resource budget	12–18 months	Option 3 (e.g. finalising)
Digital Technology	Enhance the online safety of all pupils	Triangulated approach between staff, pupils and parents to the e safety curriculum	• Less incidents of e safety issues, positive digital footprint, less pastoral concerns • Reduction of safety breaching reported via the online portal	Digital Education Lead Pastoral Staff DHT	Digital resources, assemblies, budget for parental engagement events	On going	Option 4 (e.g. complete)

And the reason I include this is because with a thoroughly thought-out and planned-out tutor time curriculum there is not one area in the box above that cannot be enhanced. It would be a very worthy activity for you to review your own school, or department involvement plan, and identify which areas of priority could be positively enhanced through an appropriate tutor time curriculum. There may be some sections of this book which will be especially useful for this. And what is more is that distilling these aims and aligning these daily aims of tutors with wider improvement goals is mutually beneficial for all stakeholders; pupils are supported to gain better outcomes in school; teachers, tutors and staff will also benefit from improved culture, attainment and wellbeing of their pupils, and perhaps even feel a greater sense of ownership over these aims and goals. This is a truly excellent opportunity to take what is already being done and tweak it in a small way to ensure quality outcomes and that the energies of staff are being channelled effectively for great outcomes. Below are documents to help you do this effectively, and blank ones can also be downloaded.

Designing a tutor time curriculum

	Aims/Intent	Action/Task	Tutor Time Action	Success Criteria	Personnel	Resource Needs	Timescale	Progress
Teaching and Learning	Increase and further develop reading attainment in Year 7	Evaluate strengths and weaknesses of current approaches resources development, teach retrieval revisit phonics where necessary		• Measure ORF aim for improvements across the year group • Assess pupil experiences of reading buddy system • Phonics testing for BAR pupils	DHT, Whole-school literacy teachers, librarian, SENCO	In-house staff coaching HTYP Resource packs Library budget Digital resources	12 months	Option 1 (e.g. yet to start)
School Culture	Develop effective corridor behaviours	Teacher a behaviour curriculum to explicitly share the desired behaviour		• Monthly reduction on corridor incidents • Improved supervising staff experiences • Sample pupil experiences across all year groups for evidence of improved experiences	DHT behaviour All school staff to reinforce	Time, School Code of Conduct, communication home, Assembly times'	12 Months	Option 2 (e.g. in progress)
Curriculum	Provide greater opportunities for 6th form pupils to engage in super curricular activities	Assess and evaluate opportunities for external events, competitions and experiences, Develop and in-house offering		• Enhanced offered of activities within each curricular areas • Sample data to assess increase uptake amongst pupils	Department heads, respective SLT, all staff. External where necessary	Staffing, budget for external events, SLT support, resource budget	12–18 months	Option 3 (e.g. finalising)
Digital Technology	Enhance the online safety of all pupils	Triangulated approach between staff, pupils and parents to the e safety curriculum		• Less incidents of e safety issues, positive digital footprint, less pastoral concerns • Reduction of safety breaching reported via the online portal	Digital Education Lead, Pastoral Staff, DHT	Digital resources, assemblies, budget for parental engagement events	On going	Option 4 (e.g. complete)

Part III
Tutor time for supporting school culture and community

Introduction

Think back to your first day working in your current school. It is likely that before you arrived for day one in your role, your decision to become a part of this institution was significant, involving substantial input from you. You likely prepared and navigated a competitive selection process to secure your position and willingly committed yourself to the opportunity, at least initially! You would have had the chance to familiarise yourself with the environment, ask questions, meet key members of staff, gather information and prepare yourself for your new responsibilities. Additionally, once in the role, you may have benefitted from a thorough handover to help ease the transition and gain a deeper understanding of exactly what the role would require of you. And on the first day, I bet you were met by someone who was expecting you, welcomed you and knew your name.

Now consider what that process is like for your pupils.

Over the last few years schools have made greater efforts to ensure there is a similar process for pupils transitioning from primary to secondary. Yet despite that, many children experience some difficulties with transition, with 1 in 4 finding it difficult (West et al., 2010). Between 2008 and 2018, more than 80% of the 96 research articles on primary–secondary school transitions highlighted the challenges associated with these transitions, noting a negative influence on academic outcomes (Jindal-Snape, et al., 2023). But the good news is that with support around 80% of young people will settle within the first few months of secondary school.

Ever-increasing demands on both school and teachers' time and resources means it is crucial that we allocate our resources effectively to prepare our pupils for this change and create capacity in existing systems rather than attempt to build new extensions into our already packed schedules. Tutors are a hugely effective lever for aiding young people as they transition through change.

Former footballer Wayne Rooney was well known for his pre-match ritual of tracking down his team's kit manager to ascertain the exact clothing items he would wear for the upcoming game. Once Wayne knew the exact items and was happy with them he would move on to the next stage of his ritualised routine: a massage and pre-game warm up. Knowing his kit items was part of his routine and enabled him to visualise and prepare for each and every element of the challenge ahead, like many other sportspeople. Like Michael Phelps and countless others, Wayne used visualisation strategies to extend a sense of control over the next challenge: mentally preparing and walking through each step of their performance has been used successfully for years.

Before the 1980 Winter Olympics in Lake Placid, researchers, funded by the Soviet government, conducted tests on athletes using four distinct training programs. These programs ranged from exclusively physical training to a blend of 25% physical training and 75% mental training. The findings indicated that performance improved in direct correlation with the inclusion of mental training, suggesting that a higher proportion of mental preparation led to better outcomes. Anne Isaac later carried out similar experiments with 78 trampolinists, some of whom were experts and others novices where she also had similar findings. Planning mentally for stressful situations can help regain a sense of control, and visualisation serves as a tool for psychological reinforcement, instilling a belief and neural pathway for success to be achieved. While this approach to mental training in isolation is unlikely to have had an impact alone, without physical training, and teamed with a wider programme, it has impacts.

In schools, we can learn from the vast expertise sportspeople have had in helping them with their preparedness. Just like Wayne Rooney, the more exposure our pupils have to specific details of their school move, the better it helps them gain an insight into what their first few days of secondary school will be like and this is a powerful tool when trying to ameliorate worries and stress about the unknown. A well-planned and intentional approach in tutor time can go a long way to supporting this.

Enabling primary pupils to meet with the tutor and key members of staff prior to transition is the gold standard of approaches. Establishing time for key introductions goes way beyond observing social pleasantries; it supports young people to build an accurate mental picture of what lies ahead, therefore freeing them to mentally prepare for it, and this enables a young person to start building a mental picture of what their school day will look like from their very first morning. This is a hugely powerful tool for supporting pupils through changes in their educational setting and can help all pupils cope with change.

This is also beneficial for tutors, and if such introductions take place in the primary school, tutors might be able to gain a greater insight into their tutees and will therefore be better informed to support them. Early instructions can support planning, therefore accommodating individual needs too, which may not be expressed in formal handover notes. In-person communication provides a host of benefits for young people and future tutors. There may also be the added benefit of gaining an enhanced handover from primary staff, who like most teachers are able to be more candid during in-person conversations rather than via formal correspondence. The seemingly minor, isolated action of meeting future pupils is a powerful step towards creating a number of very positive knock-on effects which, like dot-to-dot pictures, helps tutors and pupils start to build a picture.

A further benefit to introducing a tutor to future tutees is the greater capacity for the tutor to start learning names and give meaningful exposure to pupils. The process of learning names is often taken for granted with a faith that mere exposure or osmosis is the best process for learning names of our pupils. Yet with many teachers having over 200 pupils in their care each week, it is a task that requires dedicated effort, retrieval practice and all manner of processes we regularly apply to the learning of others. This hugely demanding task is one worth expending the energy on to get right. Creating a sense of belonging is vital for our young people in schools and the first part of this starts with being known and having teachers who recognise us and are able to call us by our names. Teachers have a host of tactics to avoid being found out when they haven't learned the names of their pupils. A study by Cooper et al. (2017) revealed the link between feelings of being valued and names being known. Early introductions enable tutors to start the process before the first day of term, and, where possible, should be accommodated for everyone's benefit. More hints and tips on this on page 45.

If you are lucky enough to get to meet future tutees in the run-up to their school transition you will want to do what you can to help them prepare, especially as some pupils may not know anyone else joining their new school. Playing icebreaker games is a great way to start, it relieves the burden from pupils, helps structure conversation and ensures everyone has a role to play. This is really positive in enabling and supporting pupils to get to know

Tutor time for supporting school culture and community

each other and you. Below are a number of Tutor time activities that can be used to help pupils prepare for transition. There are specific examples suggested but of course these are merely suggestions based on the principle of creating a supportive environment for pupils to get familiar with one another. Providing some structure to help prompt these conversations is particularly helpful when new groups come together.

These activities will also help structure introductions that may be useful for tutors who take over from a tutor at any stage too.

1 Name cards

Resources: pens, paper, and crafting items
Preparation: five minutes to collect and distribute resources
As discussed above, being known is the first step towards building a sense of belonging and comfort in your surroundings. For teachers who will see, interact with and teach easily over a hundred pupils each week it can be tricky to learn new names fast.

 Instructions
Provide pupils with cards, pens, paper and resources to their names on. Ask them to fold their paper in half so it stands up on its own. Demonstrate on the board how you can use bubble writing to add in things you like and adorn your name card with details about yourself—see image below. Give pupils 15–20 minutes to do this and let them know that this card can be placed on their desk in all lessons to help other teachers get to know them too.

 Discussion
What you do next can greatly help reinforce your knowledge of pupils' names and their interests. Discussing the pupils' work is an ideal opportunity for you to learn key details about them and their interests. This information, hopefully, will make it easier for you to remember them and their names when you come to retrieve them next time you interact. Let pupils circulate. These name cards can be used in lessons throughout the day to support other teachers in learning names as well.

 Frequency
This activity can be revisited annually.

2 Riddles

Resources: none
Preparation: none

This icebreaker works well with smaller groups or when a larger class is divided into teams of 4–5. You can also add a time challenge element to increase the excitement. In this activity, pupils are tasked with solving a riddle together. This requires communication, cooperation and problem-solving skills as they work through potential solutions.

 Instructions

Give everyone a minute or two to introduce themselves to the group and then introduce the challenge: A farmer is travelling with a wolf, chicken, and a bag of grain and arrives at a river that needs crossing. The boat can only hold the farmer and one other item. The farmer cannot leave the wolf alone with the chicken, and he cannnot leave the chicken alone with the grain. How can he safely get them all across the river?

Team members must collaborate to find a solution and then explain their thought process. For larger groups, consider splitting into teams so everyone gets a chance to participate.

Answer

- The farmer takes the chicken across the river first.
- He returns for the wolf and brings it across.
- After leaving the wolf on the other side, he takes the chicken back.
- He leaves the chicken and takes the grain across.
- Finally, he returns to get the chicken, and they are all safely across.

Other riddles such as these may also work well:

- Give me a drink, and I will die. Feed me, and I'll get bigger. What am I? A fire.
- What word begins with E and ends with E, but only has one letter? Envelope.
- What appears once in a minute, twice in a moment, but not once in a thousand years? The letter M.

Tutor time for supporting school culture and community

- What has many rings but no fingers? A telephone.
- What goes up but never comes back down? Your age.
- I go all around the world but never leave the corner. What am I? A stamp.
- If you drop a yellow hat in the Red Sea, what does it become? Wet.
- I'm light as a feather, yet the strongest person can't hold me for five minutes. What am I? Your breath.

 Discussion

At the end, ask pupils to tell each member of the group something they did well which helped the group meet their overall aim. If the group wasn't able to work it out, ask them what they would do differently next time. Offering details to structure the conversation can help pupils who may not find talking to new peers straightforward.

 Frequency

This activity can be revisited on a regular basis.

3   Jenga question and answer

Resources: Jenga games and sticky labels required
Preparation: 5 minutes to collect and distribute resources

Jenga question and answers is a fun icebreaker game which can help pupils get to know each other.

 Instructions

In small groups of 3–4, provide pupils with a game of Jenga. Explain that they will each play Jenga while answering questions. Depending on whether you have a standard or giant Jenga set, you can either write numbers that match questions or write the questions directly on each brick. You could even ask pupils to come up with these questions. When a team member pulls out a brick, they must answer the question on that brick.

With Jenga question and answer, there is an element of surprise and spontaneity, making it a relaxed and enjoyable way for pupils to learn about each other. This spontaneous aspect enhances your Jenga game beyond just stacking blocks. Questions may be designed to help pupils get to know each other or they could be a fun quick-fire round of 'this or that'.

Discussion

Ask pupils to share with the wider group something interesting that they learned about another member of the group (pupils should introduce themselves before sharing). Discussion can flow from here if commonalities are discovered, for example Callum shares that Zoe loves to play in goals at football, and asks others for their preferred positions in their sport. The aim of the game is to give pupils knowledge of each other in a memorable way.

 Frequency

Hopefully playing this game a couple of times in the initial stages of the year will be sufficient to help everyone get to know one another. Other variations which include putting topics on the Jenga blocks can be played and pupils have to talk about the issue on their brick for 30 seconds each.

4 The marshmallow/Starburst challenge

Resources: four items listed below required
Preparation: five minutes to collect and distribute resources

The marshmallow or Starburst Challenge is a fun team-building and ice-breaker game for pupils and enables them to work in smaller groups this time. Be sure to request vegan marshmallows to ensure the game is inclusive to all dietary needs.

 Instructions

Divide the class into groups of three randomly. Ideally partners should be new to each other, so instruct them to introduce themselves to each other. This activity is not just about building structures but also about learning how to work together effectively. It encourages problem-solving and creative thinking, and teamwork. Each group will need:

- 10 sticks of dry spaghetti
- sticky tape
- ball of string
- one marshmallow or one Starburst

Tell pupils that their task is to build the tallest structure they can in 20 minutes, with the marshmallow on top, using just the spaghetti, tape and string

Tutor time for supporting school culture and community

to create their structure. Provide a timeframe for the activities, 10–15 minutes should be ample. Share with pupils that their success requires teamwork, communication and creativity.

Discussion

Once the time is up, encourage pupils to reflect on their successes within the group. Offer some suggestions to help structure the conversations, for example:

- What was the most challenging part of the task?
- Did they face any initial failures? How did they recover?
- What did they think of the other groups' designs?
- What would they do differently next time?

Frequency
This should be played in the initial stages to aid transition.

5   Great Wind Blows

Resources: no resources required
Preparation: no preparation required
The Great Wind Blows is an engaging icebreaker activity that involves movement, similar to musical chairs. It encourages pupils to move around the room and reveal facts about themselves, making it a nice way for pupils to get to know one another. It is a low-pressure way for pupils to learn interesting facts about each other. You will need chairs, one less than the total number of players.

Instructions
Set up the chairs to tutor a circle, all facing inwards towards the centre. Choose one player to start in the middle. This player will stand up to begin the round.

- The player in the middle starts by saying: 'Great wind blows for everyone who . . . ' followed by something that applies to them.
- For instance, if the player has been to Canada, they might say: 'Great wind blows for everyone who has been to Canada'.

- Players who share that experience must stand up and quickly find a new seat that is more than two chairs away from their current one.
- If a player cannot find a new seat, they become the new person in the middle to start the next round.

You may wish to provide pupils with some suggested statements including:

- Great wind blows for everyone who has been to more than three countries.
- Great wind blows for everyone who hates chocolate.
- Great wind blows for everyone who has worn a onesie.
- Great wind blows for everyone who loves sushi.
- Great wind blows for everyone with a sibling.
- Great wind blows for everyone who has slept in a tent.
- Great wind blows for everyone who has a dog or pet(s).

Discussion

At the end of the game pupils should help organise the seats back as they were. Encourage pupils to find someone they have not spoken with before and talk about something they found out during this session.

Frequency

This activity can be revisited on a regular basis.

6 Collaborative drawing

Resources: creative materials, papers, coloured pencils, timer
Preparation: five minutes to gather and distribute resources

Collaborative drawing is a great icebreaker activity if there is slightly more time available. Combine everyone's artistic talents to create an ultimate drawing without seeing what others have added before. Humour is encouraged!

Instructions

Arrange pupils into groups of 4–6, ask everyone to introduce themselves and provide each member of the group with a pen or pencil and bit of paper.

- Instruct each pupil to hold their paper in portrait position and fold it in half, then again into quarter similar to folding a letter. After folding, unfold the paper so it's flat again.
- Pupils should draw a head in the uppermost section of their paper. The position and style of the head are up to them, as long as the neck connects to the top of the second section.
- Pupils fold their paper to hide the head they drew, leaving only the very bottom of the neck showing.
- Pass the folded papers to the left and accept the paper being handed from the right side.
- Each time they receive a new paper, pupils draw the missing section (torso, legs or feet) without looking at the previous sections.
- The bottom of each section should be visible to guide the next player.
- Repeat this process for the remaining sections: torso, legs and feet.
- Use a timer to keep the game moving along. Each section should have a time limit to avoid spending too long on the game.
- Once all sections are completed, unfold the papers to reveal the combined drawings.

Discussion
Encourage pupils to share the drawings within the group and say something they like about each one. The goal is for everyone to come together and enjoy creating funny and crazy creatures or characters.

Frequency
This can be revisited throughout the year, perhaps with seasonal twists.

Building social connections
While schools were first designed to ensure educational aims could be disseminated widely, the social element of school is often the most valued entity for young people. And this is not a bad thing, in fact it is essential. Social relationships have sustained humanity and are crucial for young people's healthy development. Through friendships and shared experiences and bonds, pupils learn to empathise, share resources, cooperate and explore their boundaries and social norms. Social bonds cultivate a sense of belonging and provide pupils with many things from emotional support in times of crisis to the exchange of ideas that drive innovation; social relationships sustain our humanity by nurturing cooperation, empathy and interconnectedness.

Pupils are also able to explore the expectation of social relationships and gain a deeper understanding of themselves and others. And we all know how much easier life is with friends in it.

What we know about neuroscience supports the importance of friendships during these phases of development too. During adolescence, young people go through many developmental changes, including a greater subjectification of self and the development of a stable sense of identity. Changes in the brain during adolescence, including the maturation of the prefrontal cortex, and increased connectivity between the prefrontal cortex and other brain regions involved in emotion processing, such as the amygdala and insula, enable teens to gain integration of emotional experiences into their sense of self. This impart informs their identity, and through interactions with peers, family and society, experimenting with different roles, beliefs and values, people are able to determine what resonates with them. Life is simply better with friends in it. Making friends might not always be easy but through tutor time activity we can support pupils to get to know each other, review their social connection and, where required, gain an insight into their needs. This can help tutors work with pastoral staff and highlight pupils who may benefit from social interventions. Building up a picture of your tutor tutees is an incredibly valuable method for supporting their holistic wellbeing.

Encouraging and facilitating friendships is vital for young people and their mental health too. These relationships contribute to better mental health outcomes, a sense of belonging and opportunities for learning and growth. Through interactions with peers and family, young individuals learn societal norms and values, enhancing their ability to navigate the complexities of the world around them and fostering their overall wellbeing and development. For mental health, social relationships are one of the most important protective factors, especially as pupils enter their mid (14–16 years) and late teen stage (16–19) (Högberg, 2021). So anything we can do to encourage positive relationships is of an instant benefit to our pupils as well as having a positive long-term impact.

7 Getting to know each other bingo

Resources: bingo sheets, pens/pencils
Preparation: five minutes to gather and distribute resources
With younger pupils the key is to get them talking and iterating with one another and this can be hard so it is best to find a way to scaffold the process,

and as time passes these supports can be removed. The bingo questions can be tailored to suit your specific setting, number of pupils in the class and the needs and ages of your pupils.

Instructions
Provide pupils with a bingo sheet and pen or pencil (see page 56 for a photocopiable one) and encourage them to interact with people around the room, asking questions and learning each other's names. Pupils should aim to include at least ten different names on their sheet—this will ensure they speak to a wider number of peers.

If playing competitively, advise pupils that there are three ways to win, and the first person to achieve a diagonal line, straight line and all boxes should shout BINGO.

Discussion
Once the first pupils have completed their sheet and shouted bingo, give the rest a few minutes to finish up. Then use the answers to spark discussion, for example ask if anyone else is born in March, or was anyone in the class born on the same day? Do pupils have much in common with their peers? What types of co-curricular activities might suit some of the pupils.

Frequency
Modifying the bingo games to cover essential topics and support revision will ensure this game can be revisited throughout the year in a meaningful way.

8   This or that

Resources: this or That sheets, pens/pencils
Preparation: five minutes to gather and distribute resources
Getting to know each other bingo is a wonderful game because it enables a low-pressure way of encouraging and enabling pupils to get to know each other. This game encourages communication, builds relationships and creates a fun and inclusive atmosphere for all pupils. Pupils may be more or less comfortable with it, and this enables you to divert your support to where it is needed.

Transforming Your Tutor Time Curriculum

GET TO KNOW EACH OTHER BINGO

Move around the room and ask your classmates the following questions, note down their name

who's favorite color is blue	who was born in March	who likes to eat sushi	who likes to watch TV	who has a pet dog
who likes action movies	who's favorite color is red	who has played minigolf	someone who has been to France	who likes to eat pizza
Someone who like playing rugby	who likes to draw	who's favorite color is green	who likes science	who has a cat
who has a brother	who likes maths	who plays a sport	who is as tall as you are	who's favorite color is red
who plays an instrument	who likes to paint	who has an exotic pet	who likes adventures	who has a sister

Image 3.1 Get to know each other bingo sheet

Copyright material from Kirsten Colquhoun (2025), Transforming Your Tutor Time Curriculum, Routledge.

Tutor time for supporting school culture and community

This or That

Answer the questions below with which one you prefer out of the two choices. Move around the room exploring your classmates answers for each one. How many of your peers agree with you choices?

Questions	Answers
Summer or Winter	_____
Mountains or Beach	_____
Super strength or Invisibility	_____
Reading or Maths	_____
Hot or Cold	_____
Cake or Ice cream	_____
Films or Gaming	_____
Morning or Night	_____
Dogs or Cats	_____
Chores or Homework	_____
Honey or Jam	_____
Singing or Dancing	_____

Image 3.2 This or That Activity Sheet

Instructions

Provide pupils with a This or That sheet and a pen or pencil (see page 57 for a photocopiable one). Ask pupils to partner with someone who travelled to school by the same means as them and then work through their sheets, taking it in turns to answer the questions. You may wish to do this in groups that work better for your class.

 Discussion

Once sheets are completed, encourage pupils to compare their answers and find people who are similar and different to them. You may wish to move to a floor debate and debate the ultimate question . . . cats versus dogs. Keep the discussion light and fun!

 Frequency

Modifying this game to cover essential topics and support revision choices will ensure this game can be revisited throughout the year.

9 Birthday list

Resources: access to the school database, and somewhere secure to record your list
Preparation: no preparations required

Creating a class birthday list is something many pupils will be familiar with at primary school and it can be a nice and simple way for you to get to know the class. Some online registration systems have the facility to generate a daily birthday list but if yours doesn't, or if it is less user friendly then creating your own one is a simple way to get to know the important date of the pupils in front of you. Accessing the database will also help you check in on pupils who may (believe it or not) struggle to remember their birthday when asked at random in tutor time.

It is worth noting that not all pupils will necessarily celebrate or mark their birthday in a traditional way. Jehovah's Witnesses, for example, are known to not mark birthdays in the same way as many others so this activity may not be suitable for all classes.

 Instructions

Let pupils know that your intention is to organise a birthday list, providing time for anyone who does not know their birthday to check in with you.

Challenge pupils to then line up in order of age, without using any verbal communication. Prompt pupils to use their fingers and other methods of communication to organise themselves into a literal timeline. Once this has been done, ask pupils to say out loud their birthday and check everyone is in the correct place. Then provide all pupils with a Post-it note or small bit of paper and something to write with. Instruct pupils to note their name and birthday on it. You can then add this to your calendar or online database. I like to give pupils ownership of checking for upcoming birthdays and provide resources to make birthday cards in advance.

 Discussion
Acknowledging and celebrating birthdays helps create a sense of belonging within the group. This is important for our pupils, especially when they are new to a school. Giving pupils ownership of this instils confidence and again is another opportunity for them to get to know one another.

 Frequency
This activity can be revisited throughout the year to check for birthdays and update with new pupils.

10 Spot Light

Resources: planning sheets, pens and paper
Preparation: none for the teachers but pupils will need to spend a couple of sessions preparing

Spot Light is an activity where students can share something important to them with the class. This could be an achievement, a personal interest or a 'show and tell' type of activity. The goal is to create a comfortable space for students to express themselves, build confidence and foster a sense of community within the class. This activity can be developed as appropriate to echo the outcomes and learning with classrooms. For example, this activity could be used to enable pupils to practise their public speaking skills (this may be a worthy focus ahead of speaking examinations). This is also an opportunity to visit audience expectations and discuss what good listening looks like and encourage good active listening skills. Or it could be simply used to create structures and support for pupils to get to know each other better and discover their commonalities. Ideally this would be something pupils are keen to do, rather than it being thrust upon them if they don't feel comfortable.

For older pupils you can ask them to discuss important aspects of what they would like to improve in their whole-school community, or tips on revision skills, or more reflective questions that tap into their pupil experience and provide useful information.

Instructions

The key here is to give pupils enough notice and reassurance that this does not become an onerous homework task. Explain Spot Light to the class and emphasise that this is a chance for students to have 5–10 minutes to share something important or interesting with them. When possible, let students choose their order of presentation. Some students may feel more confident going first, while others may prefer to observe first. Respect their preferences. You could set it up to prevent preparation and make thinking on their feet part of the challenge. Your choices here will depend on how well you know the class and what stage they are at.

Encourage students to choose how they would like to present their session (e.g., discussion, sharing photos and slideshow). Encourage a variety of topics for presentations: achievements, interests, hobbies, favourite books and pets. Above all, this is a chance to get to know each other better, so they should choose something they are comfortable sharing. For pupils who might be reluctant to speak, encourage them to consider the qualities of a good listener and participant (again this can be used to echo the needs of the wider school community and respond to any issues with class instruction delivery).

Depending on your workload, consider participating in Spot Light as well. Share something about yourself that students might not know (queue photos of my cute cats!).

Discussion

Encourage a positive and supportive atmosphere during presentations. Facilitate and encourage active listening after each presentation, allow time for questions or comments from classmates. Ask pupils to offer praise to each presenter. Spot Light is a valuable opportunity for pupils to share, connect and build confidence. By creating a welcoming and supportive space, you enable a sense of community within your classroom and also create an opportunity to model what it is to be a good listener and participant. Enjoy getting to know your students better through their unique and engaging presentations!

Tutor time for supporting school culture and community

Spotlight Planning Sheet

My Interest/Hobby/Topic

Interesting Details and Facts

Image 3.3 Spot Light Planning Sheet

Frequency
Depending on the reactions of your form, you could revisit this activity as often as the group wishes, perhaps discussion and agreeing different focuses for the spot lights will ensure pupils are engaged and feel and element of ownership too.

11 House time

Resources: none
Preparation: none

As mentioned previously on page 30, having a formal school-wide house system is a hugely beneficial way of organising pupils from an administrative purpose as well as a social one. Tutor time provides the perfect opportunity to share information, discuss house events and encourage pupils to connect with this part of their school life. This could be done through vertical tutors (there is more information on page 32 about how to manage these effectively).

 Instructions
Depending on the system used to organise tutor classes, this might be more or less straightforward to organise. If, like many schools, your tutor group is made up of pupils all from the same house, you may find it easier to declare your house loyalty and organise an information board in the classroom—if this is the case, involve pupils in this activity; can they create an attractive title, mascot and space for running totals and events to be displayed? If you have pupils from different houses, can you share a noticeboard? Embedding the activities and friendly competitive nature of the house system in your morning routine will help promote its importance. You may have older pupils representing the house leaders who visit your classroom and organise events; again, making sure they have the time and support to do this is important and help underscore the value the house system brings to school.

 Discussion
The important thing here is to ensure that house time is valued and its importance is clearly modelled in your classroom. Providing pupils with a way to relate to their school is a key facet to encouraging feelings of belonging. Simply sharing updates, photos and information about recent house events can be an effective way of promoting this important feature of school life.

Discussing healthy competitive spirit and appropriate behaviour is a positive way of sharing expectations with pupils.

If your timetable allows, attending house events is a great way to underline the importance of house time and get to know your pupils outside of the classroom too.

Frequency

To build up consistent and genuine connections enabling these sessions to run regularly is essential.

12 Co/Extra/Super curricular

Resources: none
Preparation: none

Another important vehicle for enhancing feelings of belonging is through the extra and co-curricular offering of schools. Studies have found that positive relationships with teachers and peers, opportunities for participation in extra-curricular activities and a sense of safety and security in the school environment are all associated with positive educational outcomes both in terms of attainment and wellbeing. For many pupils the busy school day and cycle of lessons, homework and studying can be overwhelming so creating time and space to explore the added extras of their school community is a positive and easy use of tutor time.

Finding out the details of a pupil's routines and timetable is an effective means of supporting them and assessing how well they are settling into school life. Social prescriptions can help all pupils and especially those who may be struggling to find their crowd, or need greater academic or social support. A nudge from teachers can be a useful means of getting them involved in activities which might give them the sense of belonging and positivity they need. It's all too easy for pupils to get stuck in a rut with their activities, particularly as they go through the mid-teen years and start to refine their interests and be less willing to try new things. This is where the role of the tutor can really support pupils to move in the right direction.

Instructions

Hopefully, your school has a central database, list or summary of activities available for pupils. Many schools offer activities during lunchtimes and after school. Regularly highlighting these opportunities can help pupils become aware of what's available and spark their interest in participating. Some schools expect pupils to be involved in at least two extracurricular activities. In tutor time, share these activities with your class, spend some time sharing the experiences in the class: who goes to what, and what do they enjoy about it, who would they recommend it to. Discuss the opportunities within each activity and the skills that pupils can gain.

Consider creating a survey for pupils to complete as this can also help tutors understand their tutees' interests and identify those who may need extra encouragement or assistance in finding suitable activities. On page 72, there is a suggested timetable activity to help pupils plan their free time and ensure they are not overcommitting.

Discussion

Highlighting and supporting pupils' engagement with activities outside the classroom is a key action a tutor can take to care for the whole child and ensure they have the best chance of finding something they enjoy about school. Gökmen Arslan's (2021) research, which involved a lengthy study and interviews with hundreds of school-aged pupils, adds significant evidence to an already well-researched field. This study shows that school-based inclusion and exclusion indirectly predict mental health problems through subjective wellbeing, highlighting the importance of school belongingness-based preventions and interventions to target community and wellbeing in school. The findings of this study demonstrate the role schools can play in a comprehensive prevention and intervention approach for improving adolescent mental health and wellbeing.

Connectedness is both a symptom of good wellbeing and a factor leading to it. A sense of belonging is more than just attending a group or activity with others; it is critically tied to social identity. Sharing a set of values and purpose with others creates a sense of identity. Within schools, this is a powerful vehicle for communicating desires, cultural norms and positive attributes. When used well, the activities that take place in schools outside of the classroom can enhance success in all areas of school life.

Frequency

It is important to make time to regularly check in on pupils, share news of exciting new activities with the group and encourage everyone to engage in a range of activities. I would advise doing this on at least a termly basis.

13 Routine inductions

Resources: access to school rules and behaviour conduct expectations
Preparation: none required

If belonging is at the forefront of our focus in tutor time then the first step is to share the rules, norms and expectations with pupils. This information has to be clearly communicated so pupils have a clear understanding of what is expected of them. Enabling young people to understand, access and comply with these and understand the rules and norms is a powerful step in creating a sense of belonging, calm and positive behaviour.

Using tutor time to induct pupils into their school is a good use of time and this theme may be revisited with differing focuses throughout the years as you see fit.

This will be school-specific and very much dependent on the role and routines established by your current school. For example, many schools I have worked with are increasingly developing standard approaches to corridor expectations. Crucially, this needs to be taught, not just told!

A number of schools have moved to silent corridors with the aim of improving behaviour, lessening cognitive load and providing greater space for pupils to think about their learning. These expectations and routines need to be shared, taught and fully encouraged throughout the school community. Other schools have explicit routines for leaving classrooms, entering, behaviours expected when an adult comes into the room, volume and noise levels and how to behave in a group setting like assembly. All of these must be clearly communicated to our pupils and reinforced.

Far from creating an autocratic regime, routines are hugely beneficial to both pupils' wellbeing and aiding academic activities. I suggest that creating routines is the first step to building trust and safety in a pupil–teacher relationship. Routines create certainty that can help ameliorate the stresses and worries of anxious pupils who, when presented with unfamiliarity, can struggle. Furthermore, routines and predictability in a school benefit the learning process; if we can 'free up' cognition capacity by removing uncertainty around processes and procedures, then there is more brain power for learning.

So if we want all players to do well, we must first teach them the rules of the game!

Transforming Your Tutor Time Curriculum

 Instructions

The focus may differ for you depending on the needs, age and experience of your group but I tend to focus on less policed areas where teacher instruction may not be as accessible, for example in the corridors, canteen and so on. I present pupils with a visual of the school and ask them to consider the rule (hidden and known) in each of the following domains:

- Behaviour policy
- Canteen
- Corridors
- PE department/changing room
- Assemblies
- Communication norms
- Bus behaviour
- Noise levels
- Toilets
- Break times
- Lunch times

Over the course of a weekly session we talk about the official and unofficial expectations within these areas and then revisit them as the year goes on to reinforce positive behaviour expectations. I clearly describe the actions that are required in order for them to meet the expectations; we practise them, discuss them and agree on them. Ideally schools should provide visual prompts clearly displayed in school of the desired behaviours so it is worth exploring this. Ensuring an inclusive approach is essential to support good outcomes and enable all pupils to fully access the expectations.

It is crucial that pupils fully understand the behaviour expectations and use of sanctions and also see you enacting such expectations too, so be very clear about the routines expected in tutor time!

Discussion

Providing pupils with a safe space to explore social and behavioural norms is a really important part of inducting pupils into their year group and wider school community. I tend to leave the sessions with time for discussion and questions and as the year develops and the relationships are stronger, pupils will hopefully feel comfortable asking questions and sharing their experiences with one another and the wider class. Revisit often and ensure pupils remember and understand the expectations. This makes everyone feel a greater sense of belonging and buy-in. You can consider quizzing pupils on this with cold calling techniques too to ensure they are aware and remember the expectations.

 Frequency

This session can be both proactive in helping young people adapt to their environment and the expectations, as well as being used as a means to respond to issues and concerns arising.

14 Assemblies

Resources: none, but there are many anecdotes throughout this book that can be used for assemblies if you are in charge of delivering it.
Preparation: none

Assemblies are a key component of school life, similar to routine inductions. I am writing this with a view that your role, as the tutor, is to supervise pupils while others deliver the assembly, and so your role here is to support pupils to learn and apply the expected behaviours. To ensure our pupils meet our expectations and feel confident, we must first clearly teach them what is expected. This includes guidance on behaviour, participation, noise management and seating arrangements. Most schools have a structured system for regular assemblies, and it is essential to communicate these expectations effectively to pupils.

 Instructions

It is best to introduce and reinforce the expected behaviour for assemblies at the start of the term and periodically throughout the school year. Pupils should be informed about:

- **Late arrival**
  What should they do if they arrive late? Should they enter quietly, and, if so, where should they sit?
- **Location and routine**
  Familiarise pupils with the location of assemblies. Ideally, conduct a practice session where they can go through the process of arriving, seating and participating in a mock assembly.

- **Seating arrangements**
  Ensure pupils know where their class is designated to sit, preferably maintaining the same arrangement throughout the year for consistency.
- **Clarification and support**
  Open the floor to questions, making sure that pupils understand and can comply with the expectations. Some pupils may benefit from visual aids to help them grasp these concepts. Check with your SENCO (Special Educational Needs Coordinator) if your school does not already provide these resources.

Discussion

Assemblies play a crucial role in fostering a sense of community and belonging within the school. They serve various purposes, such as religious instruction, hosting guest speakers and celebrating achievements. It is important to educate pupils on appropriate behaviour in this context, ensuring they can fully engage with the assembly without causing distractions to themselves or others. Properly set expectations help create an environment where all pupils can benefit from and enjoy these collective experiences.

Frequency

As with others, this session can be both proactive in helping young people adapt to their environment and the expectations as well as being used as a means to respond to issues and concerns arising.

15 Expectations

Resources: access to school rules and behaviour conduct expectations
Preparation: none required

Start by outlining the specific behavioural expectations in the classroom and school environment. Ideally these should be universal to the whole school and something pupils are already familiar with/aware of. It is important to be very clear and explain to pupils exactly what is expected of them. At different points in the year it is worth reviewing them, especially ahead of school trips, outings and any planned changes to the usual routine.

Instructions

Use clear and positive language to describe what is expected from pupils, for example:

- Respect: treat everyone with kindness and consideration
- Respect: the school building and facilities, move around it without causing damage
- Responsibility: take ownership of your actions and participate actively in learning.
- Safety: follow the rules to ensure a safe environment for all.

Explain why these expectations are important, emphasising how they contribute to a positive and productive learning environment. Then explicitly teach the actions that are associated with these expectations, and provide clear, step-by-step instructions. For example, if the expectation is to "listen attentively", break it down into observable actions:

- look at the speaker
- remain quiet
- raise your hand if you have a question

Encourage an open discussion about the behavioural expectations and the instructions given. Ask questions like:

- Why do you think these expectations are important?
- How do they help us learn better?
- What can we do if we find it difficult to meet these expectations?

 Discussion

Highlight the importance of following these steps consistently, explaining how it helps everyone understand and meet the expectations, and that following the rules is part and parcel of life. I often share the required behaviour for getting on an aeroplane and the consequences for failing to follow them and liken this to the school day. Demonstrating to pupils that there are expectations in all areas of life can be helpful for them to see the necessity of rules. This helps demonstrate that rules are not the result of unnecessary authoritarianism but are in place to ensure everyone's safety and wellbeing. Clear, regular communication and reinforcement is the key to helping pupil understand and recognise this.

Frequency

This session can be both proactive in helping young people adapt to their environment and their expectations as well as being used as a means to respond to issues and concerns arising.

16 Sanctions

Resources: access to school rule and behaviour conduct expectations
Preparation: none required

A good education changes lives and so it is essential that we create clear boundaries for young people to ensure that they understand how to behave in classrooms and schools. Effective behaviour management in schools hinges on establishing clear and consistent expectations. This foundation allows for a positive learning environment where teaching and learning can occur without disruptions. Tutors play a key role in this process by communicating and setting boundaries and consistently applying consequences, ensuring that all students understand the rules.

Sanctions play a crucial role in classroom behaviour management, serving to uphold behavioural expectations. They are most effective when applied fairly and consistently, with a clear understanding of the consequences for pupils. It is important that sanctions are proportional to the behaviour being addressed, maintaining a sense of justice and fairness. For this to work though, it is of the utmost importance that pupils clearly understand the sanctions in place and when they will be applied.

 Instructions

All schools should have a clear and conscious plan for ensuring positive behaviour management in schools. Ideally this should already be displayed in both written and visual forms within the schools and made available to parents and carers so they can also support it. If your school does not have a readily available guide, source one or raise it SLT so you have basis to work from in this session. Read and discuss the rules and approaches with your pupils in a way that ensures understanding. Use of explicit instruction which creates time for pupils to verbally demonstrate their understanding is a good approach. Revisit this as often as required (hopefully your electronic recording programme enables tutors to monitor the sanctions of their group).

Tutor time for supporting school culture and community

 Discussion
Sanctions have consistently proven to be effective in supporting excellent behaviour in schools. Anything that distracts from the focus on teaching and learning needs to be addressed, and using sanctions is a well-established method for achieving this. It is not the severity of sanctions, but the certainty of them that impacts behaviour. The first step in this approach is ensuring a whole-school policy that is widely known, circulated and supported.

 **Frequency**
As required!

17   Organisation 1

Resources: copies of the weekly calendar, pens/pencils
Preparation: five minutes to gather and distribute resources
Imagine an adult who is expected to attend multiple meetings throughout the day, arrive fully prepared with a detailed understanding of the minutes from the previous meeting and have completed all relevant tasks. This adult would likely have access to a personal assistant to ensure they are well-equipped to meet these expectations. Now, imagine that adult is a 14-year-old pupil carrying a heavy bag, navigating their way around a busy, bustling school while balancing the experiences of adolescence, friendship groups, extracurricular activities and various other demands. A personal assistant would certainly be useful! In reality, what these pupils have is you – an experienced adult who can guide them through the organisational challenges your subject presents. Do they have folders for each subject? Copies of their timetable? A suitable system for noting down deadlines?

 Instructions
Provide pupils with a weekly calendar similar to the one below (depending on the number of periods your school has each day), and encourage them to note down their daily classes, evening activities and plan for revision and homework time. This document should act as the foundation for their daily plans. I recommend asking pupils to take a photo of this timetable and share with their parents or carer as well as having a hard copy at home.

Weekly Calendar

	Monday	Tuesday	Wednesday	Thursday	Friday
Period 1					
Period 2					
Period 3					
Period 4					
Period 5					
Period 6					
After School					
Study Focus					

Image 3.4 Weekly Calander Template

Tutor time for supporting school culture and community

Discussion
Helping our young people with organisation is a really effective and gratifying task in Tutor Time – unlike many of the other longer term aims, here we often get to see instant results and have a full view of the positive impact we can have. Again this is a session worth revisiting throughout the year when different challenges arise; planning for school trips, exams and other busy times are all good opportunities to help our pupils gain confidence in their planning and organisational approaches. Having a list of daily classes and activities is a helpful way of supporting pupils to know where they are meant to be. It also encourages pupils to think about how they can plan their time outside of school to make sure they manage all of their opportunities and responsibilities.

Frequency
Regularly revising this task will enable young people to adapt to the demands on their time and consider how to prioritise their work. In revisiting their timetables regularly, you are better placed to pick up issues before they turn into major concerns.

18 Organisation 2

Resources: daily checklist, pens/pencils
Preparation: five minutes to gather and distribute resources
An important part of daily organisation is ensuring that pupils have their relevant equipment for each day and are fully prepared for lessons. This requirement may have also been shared as part of the behavioural and expectations lesson, and while starting the requirements is important, it is also vital we support our young people to meet them.

Instructions
Ensuring pupils are prepared for each of their subjects is a real challenge. Forgotten equipment, novels and other important items pose unnecessary distractions and interruptions at the start of lessons. One strategy to help guard against this is to encourage positive habits. Pupils should be encouraged to have separate folders for each subject and reminded to pack their bag ahead of each day, carrying only the necessary folders. It helps to involve parents in this approach too.

Depending on the ages, stage and needs of the pupil, I recommend a differentiated approach. For my younger pupils who may be straight out of primary

Transforming Your Tutor Time Curriculum

Daily Checklist

School Bag

Equipment

After School

Image 3.5 Daily Check List Template

school I recommend sharing a daily checklist with them so they start to create positive habits and approaches. Some pupils may benefit from a visual checklist and liaising with their SENCO may be a useful approach here. For older pupils, they may not need such scaffolding but perhaps gentle reminders would suffice here.

 Discussion

Being organised and prepared is a life skill and one that can hopefully be refined during the school year. If equipment needs to be borrowed, organising this during tutor time may is beneficial. However, it is much better to support pupils to manage this task themselves rather than react. Timely school bag audits may also be a useful approach here. At different times of the year pupils may need greater support with this. Later on page 76 there are suggestions for how to support pupils with exam revision.

 Frequency

As required and in response to particular needs to support the whole class and individuals.

19   Looking ahead

Resources: none other than an awareness of school events so best not done if you are a supply teachers
Preparation: none

One of the curses of knowledge we have after teaching in a school for a long time is that the many annual events which take place stop feeling so special. New pupils or Year 7s may not have nearly as good awareness as you as to the many exciting things that furnish the academic calendar. So, as part of the induction process for new pupils in secondary school, a really nice use of tutor time is to share updates and events that are happening further up the school, thus giving pupils a sense of what they have to look forward to. Each year school trips, events, tournaments and competitions will take place. Taking a little time out of the day to reflect on these opportunities and experiences can help draw awareness of the positive elements of school life.

 Instructions

Many schools today have their own portal, or social media site, where staff can submit regular updates about events and activities which have

Transforming Your Tutor Time Curriculum

taken place. Opening this up during Tutor Time simply to draw awareness, share in the excitement and discuss the benefits of these things can be a really motivating thing to do. Simply taking time to share the inner workings of school and making time for questions and discussion is a positive way to encourage participation in the wider school life and get to know your tutor class. Ask pupils to think about their own experiences and what they would like to get from a school trip, activities week or enticement courses.

Discussion

This activity serves several purposes. First, it highlights the positive and hopefully exciting opportunities your school offers its pupils, which can motivate them by showcasing the positive experiences ahead in their academic journey. Sharing the experiences of others within the school fosters a sense of connection to the wider community. Simply knowing about the significant events happening provides a sense of inclusion.

Importantly, by giving pupils the opportunity to look ahead and hopefully look forward to various activities, you are fostering a sense of hope. Hopefulness is a key protective factor against depression and anxiety – the most common mental health conditions experienced by teens. By encouraging pupils to think about and look forward to positive experiences, you help them look beyond their current situations and circumstances. Nurturing this habit and mindset can seem a small and routine action, its impacts can be far-reaching! There's more on page 108 and 110 about the power of hope and hopefulness.

 Frequency

I enjoy undertaking this session on a termly basis or as and when major school trips or events are taking place.

20-31 Fun

Resources: access to the internet and a projector, paper, pens/pencils
Preparation: five minutes to load

In building a school culture it is important to consider building in a bit of down time for pupils to decompress, relax and connect with each other over something fun. This is especially important at certain times of the year where pressures may be mounting and a fun Tutor Time session can be a welcome distraction.

Instructions

Fortunately there are a wealth of easy to use, free online platforms for quick, effortless activities in Tutor Time which can be fun and enjoyable for our pupils. Setting this up in your class will depend on the technology you pupils have. I favour playing the same (voted for) game in smaller groups to facilitate social connections and ensure no one feels exposed for not knowing the answer. I also like to tie in the games of choice to connect with wider events. For example the enthusiasm for flag-guessing games on Sporcle during sporting tournaments like the World Cup football or after the Olympics as they are more familiar with different ones.

20 Absurdle

Unlike Wordle, Absurdle is designed to be almost unsolvable. The algorithm picks words dissimilar to the player's guesses, changing the correct answer with each guess until only one word is left.

21 Artle

From the National Gallery of Art, players get four tries to identify a mystery artist by viewing four different works from the museum's collection.

22 Crosswordle

Similar to Wordle, but players solve two related words that intersect, using green, yellow, and grey boxes for guidance.

23 Dordle

Players solve two side-by-side word puzzles simultaneously, with six chances to guess both words. Options include Daily Dordle and Unlimited Dordle.

24 IYKYK

Players decipher acronyms with three guesses, receiving a hint after the second guess. It can be played once a day.

25 Nerdle

Players guess a maths equation and solution with six chances. Coloured boxes indicate correct numbers and their positions. A new puzzle is available every eight hours.

26 Octordle

Players guess eight five-letter words with 13 chances, using green and yellow squares for hints, much like Wordle.

27 Quordle

An extreme version of Wordle where players solve four five-letter words simultaneously in nine tries. New puzzles are released daily.

28 Sporcle

Pupils can access a number of geography-related quizzes. - The flag-guessing game is a particular favourite.

29 Tradle

Players guess a country based on its exports. A tree map shows exports, and guesses are guided by distance and direction to the target country.

30 Wizarding Wordle

A Harry Potter-themed Wordle with a new wizarding word puzzle every day.

31 Worldle

Players guess a country or territory from a shaded map cutout. Each guess reveals how far away and in which direction the correct country is located, with six chances to guess correctly.

Discussion

Adding fun quizzes into Tutor time offers numerous benefits for pupils, including social connections and an engaging learning environment. They are also an excellent idea for mornings when the tutor may have a busy morning ahead and needs something where pupils can work daily independently but still feel part of something. These quizzes provide opportunities for pupils to interact in a relaxed setting, helping to build friendships and a sense of community. They make learning enjoyable and interactive, motivating pupils to explore facts and details they might otherwise overlook.

By integrating educational games like Wordle, Sporcle, and other quizzes, pupils experience positive emotions, enhancing their overall school experience and promoting a positive atmosphere. This approach encourages a love for learning and cultivates an environment where pupils feel happy, engaged and connected.

 Frequency

These sessions can be integrated into regular sessions for pupils. On page 76 I suggest a weekly 'fun' session is ideal.

32-59 Annual Observations and Celebrations

An effective tutor time curriculum should be connected to the broader aims of school life. Ideally, the themes and messages delivered during tutor time should echo and support those presented in other areas of the school.

The same is true for our communities. Part of the role of the school is to ensure that pupils are able to participate in and contribute to the communities where they go to school and live. Therefore, tutor time must be inclusive of the wider issues and interests of the community. Focusing on celebrations, events and commemorations within the school community and wider society is a strong way to help pupils feel connected and more likely to develop a sense of belonging.

In the pages that follow, you will find a number of important dates as observed in the UK calendar, which may serve as a suitable focus for your tutor time. Of course, unique celebrations specific to your school, such as Founder's Day and in-house celebrations of awards and achievements, are not listed here but should be included in your unique annual plan. Below is a guide to some of the notable days currently observed. Like me, some of these may sit outside your comfort zone which is perfectly natural. Tutor time is often a short session and your main aim is to highlight these events and celebrations and spark pupils' curiosities to find out more in a meaningful way that avoids tick-box-type approaches.

Some topics you may feel tie in well to the subjects you deliver in school and so it might be worthwhile teaming up with colleagues and taking it in turns to develop different sessions. It is always worth checking in with department leads to check for cross over and replication to ensure all tutor time activities complement the wider aims of school activities.

Broken into the months of school, this section highlights some of the annual celebration and commemoration events that can be built into tutor time planning. Not many require a great deal of organisation and some may be the focus of assemblies. Although there is always a temptation to ask pupils to research different elements of these issues, people and events, I have erred away from making these suggestions. I tend to avoid asking pupils to research a new topic as their first step in learning because research shows that unguided or minimally guided approaches, while popular, are not as effective or efficient for learning. These methods can be appealing, but they often overlook how our brains process information and how students learn best. Studies from the past 50 years, including Kirschner, Sweller and Clark's 2006 work, consistently indicate that pupils benefit more from structured guidance during the learning process, especially when they are unfamiliar with the subject matter.

When pupils are just beginning to learn about a new topic, event or issue, they typically don't have enough prior knowledge to guide their own learning effectively. Without proper guidance, they can become overwhelmed, overlooked, essential concepts or simply become distracted. Given the brief time many of us have for Tutor Time, it is important to focus on providing clear instruction and support first, ensuring that the students build a strong foundation before diving into independent research. Once they have that foundation, they can, if their interest is ignited, engage in research more effectively and with greater confidence.

September

September is a busy month where many schools return after a long summer break. You may find yourself busy with induction activities and getting to know a tutor group, or settling an existing one back into the ebbs and flow of school life. September also hosts European Day of Languages and World Maths Day, and it is likely that these will be acknowledged by the academic subjects they relate to so the section below focuses on other days which may not be otherwise acknowledged. Below are some brief outlines of activities which might be suitable:

32 World Letter Writing Day

Resources: paper, pens/pencil
Preparation: five minutes to gather and distribute resources, pupils may benefit from a planning session in advance of the write up
In recent times the benefits of writing over typing has become a more topical discussion for teachers and schools. While using technology can help pupils with learning barriers, there is still a place for many to exercise their handwriting skills and knowledge of how to set up a letter.

1. This activity could be combined with the focus on gratitudes on page 128, or even for Thank a Teacher Day on page 100, an element of choice for pupils in who they choose to write to is worth considering too. It is important to support the process too.
2. First, demonstrate to pupils exactly how to set out a letter, show them where their address goes, the date and the correct salutation for each type of letter. Some pupils will be very familiar with this, others may not have a clue so support everyone through explicit teaching with scaffolds, clear instructions and an opportunity to practise and gain feedback.
3. One activity I do annually with senior classes is to encourage them to write a letter to their future (post exam) selves as a kind of time capsule-type activity. Again an element of choice is essential for this task.
4. Provide scaffolded support to pupils who may need it and provide outlines for the formatting to ensure this task is accessible for all.

33 International Day of Charity 5 September

Resources: awareness of school actions, access to the internet
Preparation: none
This one can be used to highlight the community which exists within your school. It is likely that your school already supports a specific charity or

two and today could be a nice opportunity to shine a light on who they are and what they do. If your school does not have nominated charities, then work with other tutors to identify suitable organisations that would benefit from support. Consult with SLT to ensure suitability and then on International Charity Day share details of your selected cause.

1. Discuss the existing approaches to charity within the school community.
2. Ask pupils to consider what charity really means aside from financial donations.
3. Consider sharing heart-warming stories of others who have gone above and beyond to provide charity in their community. Some notable people include: Hailey Fort, Stephen Sutton, Cassandra Gee (aka Cassie Swirls), Daniel Black, Kate McClure, James Robertson, Rachel Lapierre, Mark Bustos, Phil Packer. Searching their names alongside 'charity' should bring up their story.
4. Signpost charities which can help young people too. Depending on the age and stage of pupils it might be good to explore bursaries or grants available for pupils intending to go on to further study, or a volunteering year abroad.
5. Sharing the details of where pupils can get help during a crisis is also good. You can never do this too much:
    Childline provides a confidential telephone and online counselling service for anyone under 19. Pupils can call any time for free 24 hours days or use their website to chat to an advisor.
    The Mix provides a free, confidential telephone helpline and online service for anyone under 25.
    Papyrus (Prevention of Young Suicide) provides advice and support for young people with thoughts of suicide, or suicidal ideation, and can be accessed via their free helpline, text or email address.
    Samaritans are an organisation which can be accessed via their phone number or email address any time of the day or night

34 National Fitness Day

Resources: awareness of school actions, access to the internet
Preparation: none
Drawing attention to National Fitness Day on or around the correct date will naturally complement the aims of a good tutor time curriculum. Ensuring

positive wellbeing requires attention to be paid to the physical health and activity undertaken to support this. There is more on this on page 124 where physical health is explicitly discussed. This could be a nice opportunity to:

1. Draw further attention to the extra/co/super curricular offering of your school and encourage pupils to at least try one activity that is new to them.
2. Reflect on any recent sporting competitions and watch highlights which demonstrate resilience, bravery and determination, like the Olympics, the World Cup, US Open, Test Cricket, etc. Prompt pupils to consider the attributes of successful sports people and see if they can connect the mental attitudes required to their own life.
3. Ask pupils to share their own sporting passions with the class; this can be done like the Spot Light activity on page 61.

35 International Day of Peace

Resources: access to the internet, links with academic departments
Preparation: none

Annually, the United Nations shares a different theme for International Day of Peace. With guided activities on their website, it is worth checking in there and being cautious with this day as huge numbers of pupils identify war and threats to peace as being a particular concern they have. Other activities might include:

1. Accessing International Day of Peace websites to review the current themes and learning resources.
2. Prompting pupils to consider the wider impacts of conflict and reflect on what jobs and role they could undertake to support peace in their lifetime.
3. Link up with academic departments like History to share key information about historical issues.
4. Explore peaceful protests of the past and consider the ways people can be heard today.

October

By the time October comes around pupils should be feeling more settled into the routine of school life again but may still need support to organise their

Transforming Your Tutor Time Curriculum

workload – all ages. With half-term coming up, October can be a good time to encourage pupils to reflect on their first term at school. The following are also worth dedicating tutor time sessions to.

36 Black History Month

Resources: access to the internet, projector
Preparation: none

Black History Month is celebrated in the month of October in the UK, as opposed to the month of February in many other countries, like Canada and America. This is an important time to draw pupils' attention to the contributions and achievements of Black People in their communities.

1. Focusing on key figures who have been celebrated for their recent achievements is a great way to start, for example if the Olympics have just finished, or other events of national significance, then this is a great place to focus.
2. Use the time to reflect on why there is a need for Black History Month and how the actions of individuals matter.
3. Check out the BBC education page for a wealth of resources, short clips, timelines, articles and resources to help plan for Black History Month.

37 World Space Week

Resources: awareness of school actions, access to the internet
Preparation: none

World Space Week has a different theme each year with previous ones including Space Science and Entrepreneurship, Space Science and Climate Change, but if you are anything like me, these topics may not be ones you are confident discussing or delivering and so, for me, I reply more on external resources and pupil feedback when engaging with these types.

1. Look up online planetariums and spend time discussing the night sky – some pupils might be willing to contribute to this if this is an area of particular interest to them.

2. On the World Space Week website you can find origami activities with a space theme.
3. Look up local events and facilities such as planetariums and observatories and let pupils know of things going on in the local area.

38   World Animal Day

Resources: awareness of school actions, access to the internet, sticky notes
Preparation: none
The main aim of World Animal Day is to unite and draw attention to the global animal welfare movement to make the world a better place for all animals. This can look like many different things in Tutor Time. For me, I often start by showing photos of my adored Maine Coon cats and ask pupils about their own experience with animals.

1. Encourage the pupils to research and prepare a presentation on an animal-related topic of their choice and then host an 'Animal Mastermind' quiz.
2. You can also organise a session filled with animal-themed games. For instance, write the name of an animal on a sticky note and place it on each pupil's back. The pupils must then figure out which animal they are by asking their peers yes/no questions, such as 'Do I eat plants?' 'Can I fly?' or 'Do I have four legs?'
3. Check out worldanimalday.org.uk for a host of activities and suggestions.

39   World Mental Health Day

Resources: awareness of school actions, resources in the wellbeing section of this book, access to the internet
Preparation: none
Discussing mental health is something schools and society have made monumental progress with over the last decade. World Mental Health Day is an opportunity to draw explicit attention to this essential topic; again, signpost help and normalise its priority for everyone.

1. Many of the activities in the first part of this book are designed to support positive mental health, list writing, discussing sleep, etc., so you may

want to spend time doing one of those. Explain to pupils that the activities are designed to help them cope and thrive.
2. If it is suitable, you could arrange to take Tutor Time outside for a day and explain to pupils the positive impact being in nature can have on mental health.
3. mentalhealth.org.uk has a wider variety of suggested topics and activities too.

November
November can feel like it goes on forever. Older pupils might be getting university applications ready and may ask for time during tutor time to focus on this. Younger pupils may be feeling much more settled in to their school life and routines. It is always worth doing a check-in on how they are spending their time and prioritising workloads too. Mock exams might start being mentioned in classes and pupils should now have had multiple opportunities to practise their routines and build positive habits.

40 Armistice

Resources: awareness of school actions, access to the internet and a projector
Preparation: none
Explain to pupils an armistice is a mutual agreement between warring parties to cease hostilities. The armistice that marked the end of the First World War was signed by France, Britain and Germany on 11 November 1918, in a railway carriage in the Forest of Compiègne, about 60 km north of Paris. This agreement brought an end to a devastating global conflict that claimed the lives of millions of soldiers and civilians. The war profoundly affected people across the world, both at the time and after.

1. Share the infamous 'Lest We Forget' and encourage pupils to consider why it's important to remember and think about something so devastating – use the Think-Pair-Share. Think-Pair-Share is a collaborative strategy that encourages participation and discussion. (Think: Ask pupils a question and give them a few moments to think about their response. Pair: Have students pair up with a partner to discuss their thoughts. Share: Invite pairs to share their ideas with the class, either by speaking aloud or writing them down.)

2. Discuss the symbols associated with Armistice, the origin of the Poppy Movement, what it means and why it matters, and highlight where pupils can buy a poppy.
3. There are lots of websites with poems, articles, short clips and stories which will be ideal for Tutor Time. BBC education websites, the Imperial War Museum and the British Council are some good options.

41 Anti-Bullying Week

Resources: awareness of school rules, access to the internet and a projector
Preparation: none

The first Anti-Bullying Week started in England in 2004. Since then it has become a globally supported initiative rooted in the belief that everyone has the right to live a life free from harassment and bullying. Anti-Bullying Week is organised by the Anti-Bullying Alliance to raise awareness about the harmful effects of bullying, encourage people to take a stand against discrimination and highlight the importance of embracing individuality. It might be worth checking in with pastoral leads and year heads to find out if there are any specific issues arising within the school community.

1. Support Odd Socks Day – encourage pupils to wear odd socks which represent that everyone is different, unique and that this is to be celebrated.
2. Revisit the school rules and discuss the expectations and explicitly share what respectful behaviour looks like. Be open to discussions with pupils and guide them towards a climate which celebrates the values of inclusivity, respect and kindness.
3. Highlighting well-known celebrities who have spoken about the impact bullies had on them: Rhianna, Taylor Swift and Lady Gaga are some examples.
4. The Anti-Bullying Alliance is a very useful website with resources to help plan further activities.

December

December is a busy and relatively short month for pupils where they might be working on course work, preparing for preliminary exams and finalising their university applications. It is important to respond to these activities and support your tutees as they need it. Revisiting some of the regular expectations and routines can go a long way to supporting positive behaviour during months when holidays approach and this can be unsettling for students and cause usually excellent behaviour to slip. Gentle reminders will go a long way here.

42 International Day of Persons with Disabilities

Resources: copy of the Equality Act, access to the internet and a projector
Preparation: none
Raise awareness about the nature of disabilities, highlighting that not all disabilities are visible and not everyone may feel comfortable discussing theirs.

1. Lead a general discussion on the importance of respect and how, as a society, we must strive to create inclusive environments.
2. Explain that days like this are an important step to educating others and ensuring the aims of inclusion are never far from our minds.
3. For older pupils you may wish to explore the Equality Act and note the reasons why it's so important to have these rights enshrined in legislation.
4. Encourage pupils to reflect on their daily activities and think of ways these could be made more accessible for someone with a disability. Be mindful that this conversation may be sensitive for some pupils, so approach it with care and empathy.

43 Sports Personality of the Year

Resources: access to the internet and a projector
Preparation: none
This annual programme celebrates the success of sporting individuals and shines a light on their experiences and journey in sporting excellence.

Asking pupils to watch the Sports Personality of the Year and identify the positive qualities in the athletes helps them recognise the importance of traits such as dedication, resilience and teamwork, while also encouraging them to reflect on how these qualities can be applied in their own lives.

Tutor time for supporting school culture and community

January
As the new term and New Year begins, we have natural temporal landmarks to reset and revisit the target-setting activities on page 150. Encourage pupils to consider achievable actions for themselves and follow this up with a specific and detailed action plan.

44 Energy Saving Week

Resources: access to the internet and a projector
Preparation: none
During Energy Saving Week there are many exciting activities pupils can participate in.

1. Asking pupils to come up with creative solutions to help tackle your school's energy use will always generate a rich discussion.
2. Or simply asking them to engage in an energy-free hour at home and then share what they did with all electronic devices turned off will generate good discussion. Ask them to reflect on the experience and how they used their time differently.
3. Or consider introducing the light check challenge: pupils can check all the lights in their home and school to ensure unnecessary ones are turned off. Encourage them to make it a habit.
4. Alternatively, discussion of how pupils got to school will also generate discussion relating to energy use. Depending on the year group you could explore the different sources of energy used in your area and consider the careers and jobs related to them by way of expanding pupils' awareness of potential future careers.

45 Lunar New Year

Resources: access to the internet and a projector, creative resources for lantern task
Preparation: none
More than a billion people worldwide celebrate Lunar New Year and there are endless activities pupils can engage in to observe and learn more about Lunar New Year. These will provide an opportunity to explore a multitude

of topics, support cultural awareness, symbolism, geography, and so on. First, it might be a good idea to explore the diversity within Lunar New Year, for example across Asian countries it is celebrated in different ways, Tet in Vietnam and Solnal in North and South Korea, and Losar in Tibet. Pupils may already know some of the customs and traditions which include families gathering together for dinner on New Year's Eve, where they may enjoy special dishes that symbolise prosperity and progress, such as dumplings and fish. Elders often give red envelopes filled with money to children and unmarried people, as the red colour is thought to bring good luck. Fireworks, firecrackers and lanterns are set off to drive away evil spirits and welcome the New Year with joy. Traditional lion and dragon dances take place in public spaces, to create a festive atmosphere. Before the celebration, homes are thoroughly cleaned to sweep away bad luck, and decorations such as red lanterns and paper cuttings are put up to invite good fortune.

1. Ensure pupils have time to look up the zodiac animal for the year they were born.
2. Ask pupils to compare the symbolism noted above with symbolism in other cultural symbols.
3. Prompt and support pupils to consider why having a knowledge of other cultural celebrations is important in today's world, even if you do not observe them directly.
4. If you're feeling really creative, ask to help tidy your classroom then download simple lantern designs from the internet and ask pupils to help decorate your classroom.

46 Martin Luther King Day

Resources: access to the internet and a projector
Preparation: none
Most pupils will likely have some awareness of Martin Luther King, and it is possible that the history department may already have plans to commemorate him on this day. It would be beneficial to consult with them to ensure that your activities complement others taking place across the school.

1. A good starting point is to provide pupils with a brief introduction to who Martin Luther King was, what he stood for, and why he continues

to be celebrated today. Showing a clip of his iconic 'I Have a Dream' speech, followed by encouraging pupils to write down their own hopes and dreams for a more peaceful and fair world, can be a meaningful way to honour his legacy.
2. Other activities could include sharing some of his famous quotes and having pupils consider their significance and compose their own.

Prompt pupils to share details with one another of other role models they know of. If you are with your tutor group for a number of years, you may wish to ask them to take ownership of annual days like this and come up with a selection of activities they would like to do.

February
February is a shorter teaching month with lots of progress being made with course delivery and it is likely your pupils will have received a report on their progress. Setting time aside to review will be a great use of tutor time but just be careful to make sure pupils are supportive of this as some may feel exposed and disappointed with their grades and may not be open to wider discussions. Tips to keep this positive and on track can be found on page 152. As well as the two focus areas below, February also sees the celebration of International Day of Girls and Women in Science and National Engineers Week which may well be commemorated (celebrated?) within those academic subject areas.

47 Children's Mental Health Week

Resources: activities and resources in the wellbeing section of this book, access to the internet and a projector
Preparation: none
This is an important week-long focus on children's mental health. Depending on the activities you have already engaged with from the first part this would be a good time to allow pupils to select the activities they would find meaningful.

1. Other options include supporting discussion about well-known sports stars, or celebrities who are speaking out in support of Children's Mental Health Week and consider why it is so important to have awareness of these role models.

2. A fuller selection of options can be found from page 101 onwards. It is always a good idea to revisit where a pupil can get further help from, should they need it as discussion on page 126.

48 Safer Internet Day

Resources: access to the internet and a projector
Preparation: none

Safer Internet Day has become more and more important and even critical for everyone in recent years with a host of activities being made available online to support pupils making positive choices in their online lives. Today would be a good time to revisit any in-house guidance around the use of mobile phones and computers at school. Sharing details of the moon landings and permanency of Buzz Aldrin's infamously photographed footprints is a good way of promoting pupils to frame the permanency of their own digital footprint. In talking about e-safety it is vital not to demonise screen time and the internet but guide pupils towards exploring the possible pitfalls and arm them with the guidance in how to avoid common mistakes like sharing offensive information, (accidentally) sharing personal or sensitive information such as financial details. Regular, thoughtful approaches to e-safety help prevent pupils from developing a false sense of security due to the screen, ensuring they don't make mistakes online that they would not in face-to-face interactions. Other activities include:

1. Planning their screen use and time allowances are also good ways to focus on positive behaviours.
2. Provide links to e-safety websites (such as Childnet or CEOP) and have pupils explore them or do the quiz together.
3. Discuss and challenge pupils to create strong passwords using a mix of letters, numbers and symbols. Discuss the importance of unique passwords and how to manage them safely.

March

March sees a huge number of days of note: International Day of Happiness, Women's History Month, World Book Day and Young Carers Action Day, British Science Week and many more. It might be worth sharing with your pupils that although we live in a time where we have a greater awareness and understanding of gender differences, similarities and neutrality, historically females have not experienced this, and so many of these days are designed to shine a light on those whose journeys and achievements have been hindered. It is important to explain to young people the origins of these days and weeks of note in an informative and inclusive way to support the development of inclusion and diversity,

49   World Wildlife Day

Resources: none
Preparation: none
Is a lovely opportunity to take tutor time outside and if feasible have a walk around the campus to see what flora and fauna you can find. This serves as a reminder to ensure adequate time is spent outside, benefitting from the fresh air and regular role that sunshine plays in getting enough sleep.

1. Other activities include playing wildlife hangman in groups.
2. As a class, finding out more about local conservation efforts and considering how the school community can help.

50   Brain Awareness Week

Resources: activities and resources in the Wellbeing section of this book, access to the internet and a projector
Preparation: none
Brain awareness week is an ideal time to explore the ways to keep the brain healthy. Activities earlier in the book, discussions regarding sleep and exercise needs will complement this week well. Additionally, the activities on page 155 discuss the neuroscience of the brain and learning will give pupils a fuller understanding of the reasoning behind teaching approaches. Encourage pupils to choose two good brain habits this week, and reflect on the impact making good choices can have on overall wellness. There are also a host of activities available on various platforms to show pupils the brain and learning in action. Depending on the year groups involved and the knowledge of human biology, more challenging articles should be made available to explore this.

51 Neurodiversity Celebration Week

Resources: activities and resources in the Wellbeing section of this book, access to the internet and a projector
Preparation: none

This is an area of increasing importance as we in society become more aware of the diversities which exist. This week could be a good opportunity to dispel any myths that can surround neurodivergence.

1. At the start of the week as pupils to note down any questions they have about neurodivergence, then vet the questions, once you have had a chance to do this (just in case!), invite one member of the SEN team or SENCO to answer some of the questions.
Involving pupils in the content being discussed can help build towards a more inclusive and accepting school environment.
2. Following on from this discussion, ask pupils about the actions they can take to ensure their actions are inclusive and agree on three for the whole class.
3. Revisit this and reinforce it regularly so this does not become a tick-box exercise tied to one week of the year.

52 National Poetry Day

Resources: poems access to the internet and a projector, papers pens/pencils
Preparation: five minutes to organise and distribute resources

It is highly likely that the English department will have this covered, however there is a nice opportunity to get creative and combine this with national happiness day. Get pupils into groups and ask them to compose a short poem or even Haiku about happiness. Share your own too. Other activities could involve exploring your own favourite poems or opening the floor and asking pupils for theirs and setting a memory challenge to see if anyone can recite a poem.

April

April is a quick month most often broken up by the Spring holidays. With less time available it is important to really consider the needs of your tutor group and don't be afraid to edit and change your tutor time curriculum accordingly. You may also have had greater whole-school communication regarding current issues or priorities for the school community, for example if there has been an increase in incidents of bullying or data demonstrating a lag in certain subjects, you can use Tutor Time effectively to contribute to the response. There are some important days of note in April including a month-long celebration of Mathematics Awareness Month, World Autism Week, and Shakespeare's Birthday. Again it is highly likely that the academic subject areas will visit some themes.

53 National Pet Month

If you have been a tutor to your group since they joined in Year 7, you likely already know about any special pets in their lives, or perhaps allergies or reasons they may not have pets, which can be a sensitive topic for some pupils.

1. To avoid repetitive conversations about which pupils have cats and dogs, it might be helpful to explore some well-known stories of animals and their owners. I often use anecdotes and stories to reinforce key points because, as humans, we naturally connect with narratives where we can empathise and understand the role of emotions and feelings. Pupils are no different, so using notable stories of animals and their owners to illustrate kindness can be an effective tool to create calm and inspire kindness in the school community without making the discussions too personal.

    One such story to do that is the touching memoir of Greyfriars Bobby. Bobby, a small terrier, became known for staying by his master's grave for 14 years after his death. His owner, John Gray, had worked as a night watchman and later passed away in 1858, before being buried in Greyfriars Kirkyard, Edinburgh. Despite no longer having a home to go to, Bobby refused to leave the graveside, instead sitting on his master's grave, and leaving only to find scraps of food. According to the now legend, locals took care of him, and he became a symbol of unwavering loyalty.

    Later when laws were introduced to require dog's owners to have a licence for their animals, Bobby, as a stray, faced being put down, but the Lord Provost of Edinburgh paid for his licence, thus enabling Bobby to stay near his master's grave. Bobby later passed away in 1872 and was buried just inside the cemetery gates. Bobby's story has since become part of Edinburgh's folklore where he is celebrated as a symbol of loyalty, with a statue erected in his memory, now rubbed for luck. It is a beautiful reminder of the bond between humans and animals.

Share this tale and others you may know with pupils and ask for any similar stories they know of love and loyalty between animals and people.

2. Alternatively, and if you are anything like me, you could easily spend the whole week showing photos and talking about your own adorable cats if you are lucky enough to have them! Modelling and explaining the joy individuals can take from small things and pets they care about is an important part of developing empathy and understanding in young people, so even if they are not animal lovers this activity serves an important purpose.

54 Allergy Awareness Week

Resources: activities and resources in the Wellbeing section of this book, access to the internet and a projector
Preparation: none

Drawing awareness to this can be a good follow-on from the discussion on pets and animals. Your school may well have a specific allergy policy and now, before the summer term, which often has trips and activities planned, would be a sensible time to revisit it and ensure pupils understand which foods they are asked not to take into school.

1. Allergy Awareness Week has a number of web pages dedicated to raising awareness and educating people about the impact, symptoms and consequences of allergies. It is worth visiting them and sharing some of the lived experiences on the website.
2. Other activities could include spending time on the St John Ambulance website to view the actions and help sometimes required when someone experiences an allergic reaction. Done well, this can reassure pupils that there are a host of plans and policies in place should anyone need help.

May

May is likely to be a busy month with exams looming and pupils' activities and adventures being planned. There are less days of note to consider adding in here so more time might be spent reviewing any changes to sleeping patterns as the light nights become more established, and considering reviewing the goals and aims set out in January. Effective revision strategies might also be a sensible inclusion this month,

55 Mental Health Awareness Week

Resources: activities and resources in the wellbeing section of this book, access to the internet and a projector
Preparation: none
Littered throughout the calendar year are these poignant reminders that mental health matters. Starting with a point of highlighting the frequency within the year these dates appear could generate good discussion about why it is so important to keep conversations about mental health a regular occurrence.

1. Many of the activities already covered can be used to reinforce good methods of looking after ourselves.
2. Revisiting previous discussions, aims and intentions will continue to ensure they are done with meaning and not as add-ons, or tick-box activities.
3. Other activities can be found on many mental health awareness week websites.
4. Additionally, it would be worth checking with the Pastoral Lead to see if anything in the PSE curriculum could be revisited and reinforced through Tutor Time.

56 National Walking Month

Resources: activities and resources in the Wellbeing section of this book, access to the internet and a projector
Preparation: none
This focus provides a great rationale for revising the importance of physical wellness and health for any aspects of overall health. From getting adequate daily exposure to sunlight for sleep health, to staying fit through physical exercise is vital for overall wellbeing.

1. If it works for your location, taking Tutor Time outside is a lovely way to observe this week.
2. Alternatively, discussing well-known local walks of interest and drawing pupils' awareness of the importance is useful.
3. If your school has a co-curricular walking group, inviting someone along to showcase the group is another way of strengthening community bonds within your school and encouraging pupils to try something new,

June

By June the summer is fast approaching and pupils will be finishing up topics, units of learning and their exams. You may have more time available if you benefit from study leave. Hopefully this should be a welcome decline before the break arrives. June is home to a number of important days of note, including World Environment Day and Oceans Day, Refugee Week and Thank a Teacher Day.

57 Pride Month

Resources: access to the internet and a projector, creative resources
Preparation: none

Pride Month is an important part of any school calendar and deserves to be recognised as such. However, as with many significant celebrations and commemorations, it is crucial that these days, weeks and months serve to highlight and celebrate the ongoing work being done throughout the school year. We should never rely on these specific times as the sole moments to acknowledge these issues. It is not about ticking boxes but about ensuring these values are embedded into our practices all year round, so it is worth considering how you could embed the themes of equality, love and campaigning within the tutor curriculum.

As with all of these themes, as you are with your class for longer you may wish to give them greater autonomy to celebrate and observe these dates in a way that they feel works well. Other activities include:

1. Introducing pupils to the history of Pride Month by providing a brief lesson on the history of Pride, covering significant events and the evolution of LGBTQ+ rights. This could be paired with a short video or slideshow

found on many reliable websites to help observe Pride in age-appropriate ways.
2. Facilitate discussion of LGBTQ+ Role Models highlight influential LGBTQ+ figures across various fields (science, literature, sports, etc.). Pupils can research and present on figures such as Alan Turing, Marsha P. Johnson or Nicola Adams.
3. Introduce the Pride Rainbow flag and discuss the symbolism. Explain allyship and design flags or rainbows to celebrate the uniqueness of your school community.

58 Refugee Week

Resources: access to the internet and a projector
Preparation: none

Refugee Week is a global festival celebrating the resilience, creativity and contributions of refugees and those seeking asylum. Established in the UK in 1998, it is an extension of World Refugee Day, which is celebrated on 20 June. Refugee week features a wide range of events including art exhibitions, and educational activities, all aimed at building understanding and connection between communities. This week is about more than simply acknowledging refugees; it is a chance to develop empathy, challenge misconceptions and recognise the positive impact refugees bring to society.

1. Raising awareness during Refugee Week is a valuable way to highlight and celebrate the resilience, contributions and creativity of refugees around the world. However, it is important to remember that this is a moment to highlight these things and is not the only time we should be curious, empathetic and supportive of people seeking sanctuary. Building understanding and connection should be ongoing, extending well beyond the week itself. There is a plethora of resources on the official website where classes can watch short clips, enjoy visual arts and learn more. Spending some time exploring the words:
   - Refugee
   - Asylum
   - Persecution
   - Migrant
   - Displacement

- Resettlement
- Internally Displaced Person (IDP)
- Humanitarian Aid
- Trauma
- United Nations Refugee Agency (UNHCR)
- Nationality
- And defining them is an important step. Doing this as in Tutor Time is an excellent way to ensure all pupils are made aware of this important week.

59 Thank a Teacher Day

Resources: creative resources, paper, pen and pencil
Preparation: none

As the term draws to a close, it is the perfect time to practise gratitude by pausing to appreciate those who have supported us along the way. In this session, encourage pupils to reflect on the teachers and staff members who have made a positive impact on their lives. Ask them to think of someone they would like to thank and write a short note, card or email expressing their appreciation.

Begin with a quiet moment of reflection, invite pupils to consider something meaningful a teacher has done for them. Afterwards, encourage a few to share their thoughts if they feel comfortable. This reflective activity allows pupils to recognise and celebrate their teachers' kindness in a personal and thoughtful way.

Part IV
Tutor time for health and wellbeing

Pupil wellbeing is my passion, my previous book, *Pupil Wellbeing*, was a labour of love and was written with the intention of creating a practical guide for classroom teachers, all of whom hold a great deal of influence over the wellbeing of pupils. While researching for that book I read hundreds of articles, publications and books, many of which presented their own unique definition for wellbeing.

Health and wellbeing are central to a teacher's responsibilities, carrying significant accountability. In the United Kingdom and globally, schools play a crucial role in addressing a wide range of social, emotional, physical, mental and increasingly financial challenges faced by students, in addition to their academic pursuits. Schools' roles extend beyond academics to include cultural transmission and guiding students into adulthood. Implementing effective health policies in schools promotes healthy behaviours during and beyond school years.

Despite legislative details, curriculums and inspection procedures, how we observe the health and wellbeing of pupils can be hugely subjective. What looks like wellness to you may not be shared by those colleagues practising in neighbouring classrooms. Subjective wellbeing and eudaimonic wellbeing are often the ones we really mean when we are considering pupil wellbeing, that is, how an individual feels about themselves and their lives.

For educators, I prefer a much more practical definition and consider wellbeing to be a seesaw. Challenges are inevitable and will come in many different forms for our pupils, learning barriers, grief, stress and so on, but at the other end we have our resources, our school systems which are adaptable and can offer unique responses to the challenges being faced. I suggest that a persons' wellbeing exists when there is a healthy and effective balance between the challenges and resources available to a young person. It is never the responsibility of a teacher, pastoral lead or tutor teachers to be responsible for waving a magic wellbeing wand and dissolving all the

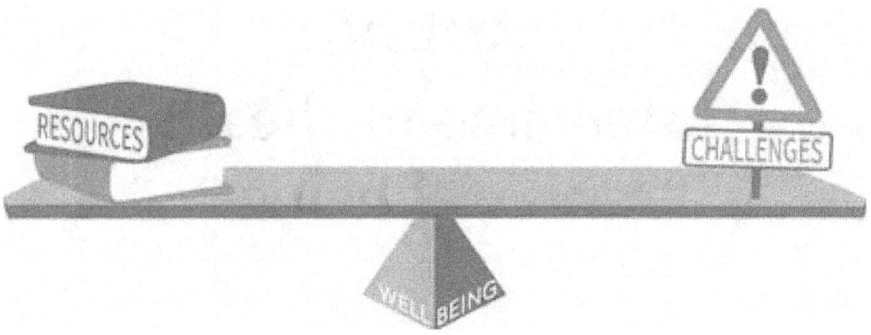

Image 4.1 Wellbeing Seesaw

challenges facing our pupils. Such a belief is a contributor to why we have issues with teacher burnout.

As political ideologies shift and society evolves, education often becomes a frontline response. Changes in curriculums, teaching philosophies, pedagogical methods and teacher workloads are common as schools adapt to new demands. Teachers face numerous challenges, balancing the need to improve local authority league table standings, meet parental expectations for academic success and fulfil political goals, as seen during the pandemic. Additionally, teachers strive to address each student's unique needs, seeking assistance from other professionals when necessary. Despite these challenges, the UK benefits from many dedicated, successful teachers and a progressive approach to education and research.

In researching, writing and working within the wellbeing space I am frequently asked why the wellbeing of young people should fall on the shoulders of teachers and school leaders when really their aim is to enhance the academic abilities of the pupils. And I understand the argument, teachers are busy people with huge demands upon them, yet it is critical to not view the two endeavours as a dichotomy: we should recognise that they are two sides to the same coin. The data unequivocally demonstrates that wellbeing and academic attainment are mutually beneficial and indeed one enables the other. A good education has the power to change lives and we know positive wellbeing makes this accessible to so many young people. Equally, we know that a good education creates a greater likelihood of having positive wellbeing ratings later in life and so I argue that they are both a key priority within the modern education system.

It is abundantly clear that there is no shortage of publications on wellbeing in education, and as a key facet of education, it is here to stay. Developing the health and wellbeing of our young people is not driven by the sole motivation to increase attainment but rather to provide and enhance them with the skills, knowledge and resilience to lead happy and healthy lives. Better educational outcomes impact positive life experiences.

The challenges are real and vast. Post-pandemic there is wide discussion about the impact change had on our education system. However when we examine data it is evident that young people have been facing a multitude of challenges which predate COVID-19. The pandemic has served to highlight the need for effective guidance, wellbeing support and care in education. PISA (Program for Internation Student Assessment) Data and the Good Childhood Report (2024) all highlight major concerns relating to the health and wellbeing of young people today and the latter highlights a concerning trend: many young people are dissatisfied with their lives. According to our household survey conducted in May and June 2023, 10% of children aged 10 to 17 reported low wellbeing, and nearly a third expressed unhappiness with at least one specific aspect of their lives.

Education in the United Kingdom is a devolved responsibility, with each of the four nations having its own policies, priorities and direction. However, they each share a deep-rooted commitment to deliver and prioritise pastoral care. The idea that education might deliver social, emotional and health care was suggested as early as the 1900s and has been cemented within the various curriculum models since the 1970s. Below are a number of activities which can be used in conjunction with the personal, social and health curriculum.

Within British schools, as in many other parts of the world, there are clearly defined roles for pastoral leads. Responsibility and authority are given to heads of year, heads of guidance and pastoral leaders. These leadership structures ensure personal, social and health education are effectively delivered; that safeguarding practices are in place; and that there is a connection between the education sector and the external agencies that play a role in keeping children and young people safe. Welfare, however, is the responsibility of all teaching colleagues. Being a teacher of health and wellbeing is an expectation that is required for all teachers, and indeed all those who work with young people.

This approach is effective and creates a safety net for young people, it ensures that there is designated responsibility for safeguarding, delivering key personal, social and health education as well as encouraging positive relationships. However, the volume and frequency of a tutor contact with their set creates an undeniable opportunity for schools to complement the actions taken to enhance the wellbeing of pupils. The following activities suggest approaches that can be used to help create effective environments and support the vital work schools do to promote positive wellbeing.

As with anything in schools it is vital for all staff to remember that they are not working alone. In helping to encourage positive wellbeing, Tutors need to work closely within the wider aims of the school. As a tutor your role here is to support the wider wellbeing activities, themes and issues being raised and discussed within the PSE curriculum and year groups. Tutor Time offers a chance to revisit key themes and ideas in a way that drip feeds them into a pupil's awareness. Working within the team of staff, consulting with guidance teachers, Year Heads and those with strategic responsibilities is essential when thinking about the role of the tutor and the actions they can take to support young people.

As mental health and wellbeing has become a more pressing issue for young people there has been a natural desire to find actionable responses to help our young people. So what you won't see on the following pages are mindfulness approaches or strategies. As a promoter of being evidence-informed it is vital for me to ensure all the activities and ideas I share are *fully* backed by evidence and proven to be effective and therefore worthy of your time and effort.

Mindfulness activities are a good example of well-meaning, logical approaches which are frequently invested in and offered within our schools but for which there is a lack of firm evidence regarding effectiveness.

Unfortunately, our propensity in education is to have good ideas thrust upon us which has resulted in a whole economy of wellbeing, and as Professor Kuyken of the MYRIAD trial has stated: 'enthusiasm was ahead of the evidence'. So until the long-term benefits of mindfulness approaches are proven, I would strongly argue that we should invest time and effort in the long-term strategies more akin to the approaches James Brailford took and stick to what we know works.

60 Wellbeing check-in

Resources: none
Preparation: none

Prioritising a regular wellbeing check-in is a reliable way of enhancing our pupils' emotional literacy. In doing so we are creating the time, space and support for pupils to reflect on their lives and assess how they feel about things. It also demonstrates to pupils that someone cares, someone will take

Tutor time for health and wellbeing

time and energy to check in with them. This is a worthwhile activity in itself but also serves to create better self-awareness and can act as a prompt for Tutors to flag any concerns to relevant pastoral staff and year heads. If your school has a clear and workable definition of wellbeing (and I hope it does), then it is worth using that shared language in these check-ins.

Encouraging regular check-ins also encourages pupils to reflect on where they are now compared to previously; this can highlight positive resilience or highlight a need for further support. During stress points within the year this reflection may highlight a need for assemblies on study skills, greater support for homework and even a need to take a constructive approach to discussing challenging current events. In seeking out information from these check-ins, the tutor is able to take an actionable next step both for individuals and whole classes, where the need is identified.

A further benefit of encouraging pupils to reflect on their own mental states is that this promotes awareness now and hopefully for life. As a tutor you are being proactive in order to ensure your pupils' wellbeing can be maintained positively and is supported.

Quite simply, you are telling, showing and modelling that how they feel matters and someone is always listening. This is a hugely important message and one we should all support.

Instructions

Share the rationale of what you're doing and why. Pupils should clearly understand that how they feel matters, they have a right to be happy, healthy and supported.

1. Ask them to consider how they feel today on a scale of 1 to 10 (1 being awful, 10 being wonderful).
2. Pupils do not need to share this or discuss it out loud – some schools may have a section within their homework diary system for pupils to record this so encourage them to do so if appropriate.
3. Once a pupil has considered where they are on the scale, ask them to consider where they are normally. Give time for this and encourage inner reflection here.
4. Ask pupils to think about their two numbers and consider factors which might be impacting them to be either similar or different.
5. Encourage pupils to reach out for help if there is more than a two-point disparity between the two numbers.

Discussion
Building this into tutor time supports the creation of a positive habit and enables pupils to set aside time for personal reflection. These sessions can support wider initiatives within the school and are especially important during difficult times. Signposting websites where pupils are able to speak to someone in confidence is a worthy activity. Childline has a fantastic wealth of resources to support young people through many stages of adolescence. Sharing the details of how to access help and information via the site can help de-stigmatise mental health. It is also to highlight that platforms like Childline are not just for times of crisis.

Encouraging pupils to talk about their reflection is optional and through chatting with you, the tutor teacher can model this and hopefully create the climate for pupils to feel that they are in a supportive environment and know the route and pathway for help.

 Frequency
This activity can be revisited on a regular basis to prompt pupils to reflect on their wellbeing and know that you are there to support them.

61 Stress and worry

Resources: none
Preparation: none
Having open discussion about what stress is, why we feel it and how to ensure it stays in the positive zone is an effective way of improving emotional literacy and looking after our pupils. The most common drivers for teen stress are their relationships with peers and families, and exams. These factors play a huge role in a young person's mental wellbeing, so it is vital that we make time to discuss, normalise and help young people out with these feelings.

When speaking with young people I am always mindful to use the terms 'worry' and 'stress' as opposed to the often overused 'anxiety'. With pupils it is important that we normalise feelings of worry and stress but give them the tools and guidance to ensure that these feelings are within the bounds of normal responses to environmental pressures. For example, it is normal, healthy even, to worry about exam results. It is OK to feel stressed out about a public speaking event. What is not OK is if these feelings persist and start to appear in anticipation of potential events. This is where anxiety can start to develop. The Harvard Center for the Developing Child outlines three categories of stress: positive, tolerable and toxic. Positive stress, such as the pressure to study and improve, can be beneficial, fostering resilience and coping skills. Tolerable stress, although temporary, can be managed with support and resilience. However, toxic stress arises from prolonged stress without adequate support, posing significant risks to mental and physical health.

 Instructions

1. Ask pupils to identify events, issues or times that make them feel stressed or cause them to worry. Encourage them to reflect upon the reason behind these feelings and to consider that sometimes these feelings can be positive. Highlight that the difference between motivational stress and chronic stress is how long these feelings last and how well placed we feel to respond to them, do we have the knowledge, resources and help?

    Share this with pupils.

    Or, depending on the age of pupils you could go further and explore The Yerkes-Dodson curve, which is a psychological concept that shows the link between stress levels and performance. It suggests that performance improves as stress or arousal increases, but only up to a certain point. Beyond this, too much stress causes performance to decline. In simpler terms, a moderate amount of stress can boost focus and efficiency, but too much leads to anxiety and reduced performance. For teachers, this means creating a balanced learning environment that challenges pupils without overwhelming them. Pupils can also apply this idea when organising their commitments, revision schedules and homework strategies. Drawing awareness to this and providing pupils with a chance to be self-aware can help them both now and in the future.

2. Highlight where and how pupils can get help. For example, if many of your pupils identify maths tests to be a major cause of stress, suggest attending maths clubs or homework clubs if it is offered. If pupils have general worries and concerns, remind them of the help they can get from staff, their guidance teachers, parents and other trusted adults. Signposting the services offered by Childline, who offer a host of help and advice for young people, not only during times of crisis.

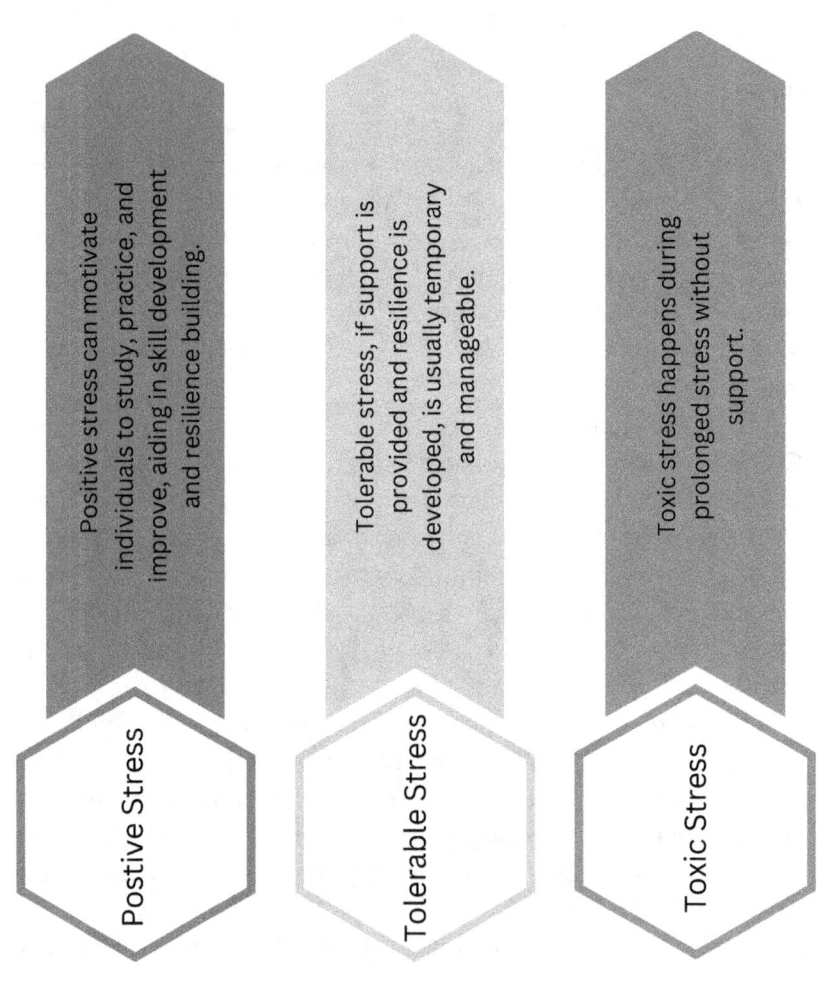

Image 4.2 Stress Traffic Lights

Discussion
Simply hosting a discussion about stress, worry and mental health is a powerful action that signals to young people that these issues matter. It is important to revisit these themes and issues as and when the needs arise. Working in conjunction with guidance staff and year heads to be proactive ahead of exams or known pressure points is an effective way to support young people. Again the focus here is little and often, with sign posting pupils towards further help, if required.

62

Resources: access to the internet and a projector
Preparation: % minutes to research and source quotations

Hope 1

Ask anyone who dares to believe in the Scottish national football team and they will tell you that the key is to remain hopeful. Supporting the Scottish national football team is the ultimate act of optimistic resilience. Against all logic, history and experience, we choose to believe. Every heartbreak kick-starts the process of picking ourselves up, and somehow, we always decide that tomorrow could be *our* day, no matter how much the past says otherwise! It is not just football; it is a lesson in unshakeable hope. Hopefully that one day is our day. The same can be said of supporters of many sports, or even anyone who has ever relied on the British Weather. Hope and our faith in things improving is a powerful tool which helps us move beyond the current challenges we face.

Hope and hopefulness play significant roles in mental wellbeing by influencing various aspects of psychological and emotional health. Hopeful people are better at coping with stress and adversity, viewing challenges as manageable and believing in their ability to find solutions, which reduces feelings of helplessness and anxiety. There are a number of reasons to consider building sessions on hope and hopefulness into your tutor time curriculum; through focusing on hope, pupils are encouraged to view the futures in a positive light. This can encourage pupils to think beyond their current worries and stressors and can support them to improve their mental wellbeing, and promote a positive and fulfilling life.

Instructions

Introduce the session and ask pupils to define what hope means to them. Once pupils have roughly settled on a meaning, open the floor to discussion and get feedback about their ideas on hope.

Display or project ten quotes about hope, for example:

Emily Dickenson, George Washington Carver, Aristotle Desmond, Tutu, Martin Luther King, Thich Nhat Hanh, John Lennon and Christopher Reeve also have some good quotes about hope which can be found on Google.

If you feel comfortable sharing, like the point I made above about being a Scottish Football supporter, share something you feel hopeful about and ask pupils to reflect on something they have faith will be better, or come to fruition in the future.

 Discussion

The main aim of this session is to open the gates to discussing hope and hopefulness. You may want to time this session around challenges pupils are facing, such as during the build up to exams and other pressure points in the year. The key is to start providing pupils with the building blocks for a positive mental outlook, with hope being a foundational element. The discussion may not progress very far depending on how it unfolds, but it is important to allow the conversation to flow naturally and meaningfully. This session is meant to complement broader discussions about mental outlook and support the wider aims of the school.

 Frequency

This activity can be revisited on a regular basis.

63

Resources: paper, pens/pencils
Preparation: none

Hope 2

Hopefulness is a powerful disposition which enables us to look ahead of our current woes, build resilience and enhance emotional health. Hopefulness and hope encourage goal setting and a belief in improvement which can provide motivation and a sense of purpose, leading to accomplishment and fulfilment. It is closely linked to resilience, helping individuals recover from setbacks and

Tutor time for health and wellbeing

maintain mental health. Additionally, hope acts as a protective factor against mental health disorders like depression and anxiety, and fosters creativity and effective problem-solving. Overall, hope enhances life satisfaction by encouraging a focus on positive possibilities and outcomes.

Instructions
Explain to pupils the impact of hope on their mental wellbeing. Encourage pupils to reflect on their hopes and aspirations for the coming year. If they are willing, provide pens, paper and envelopes for them to write a letter to their future selves. Prompt pupils to consider their current challenges and envision how their future selves will have overcome them, reflecting on happy experiences and achievements they anticipate.

I have done this activity with pupils for many years, and I typically keep these letters for about a decade before returning them at a school reunion. Whether you choose to retain the letters or have students keep them, shifting their focus towards the future helps guard against feelings of being trapped or stuck in present concerns, fostering a sense of hopefulness.

Discussion
Regardless of the chosen timeframe for returning their letters, this task encourages pupils to see their current situation as temporary. While young people may sometimes feel overwhelmed by current challenges, teaching them to cultivate hope is a profoundly empowering tool for their future. Understandably, a single lesson alone cannot entirely shift mind-set, but explaining the purpose of this activity is a small yet significant step towards helping students develop the invaluable perspectives of hope and hopefulness.

Frequency
This activity can be revisited annually or termly.

64 Workload check

Resources: none
Preparation: none
Linked closely to stress, it is important to check in on pupils and actively help them find strategies to manage their workload and commitments. Encouraging pupils to join in with activities and make the most of the opportunities available to them is an important part of a tutor's role. The other side

of that coin is ensuring that they are not *overly* committed. During my time in schools, I observed that there are pupils who are more at risk of this than others, however the shifting demands throughout the years makes it a topic worth exploring with all pupils.

 Instructions

It can be difficult for everyone and especially teens to take a step back from their daily lives and assess their workloads. During this task it is important to use a social story or model to illustrate the need to take stock of their time, or to reflect. I often do this through discussion of the approaches someone might take to marathon training. I share with pupils that if a novice runner wanted to compete in a marathon they wouldn't start off by training to run the full 26+ miles each day. We explore what the consequences of this would be – fatigue, injury, and so on.

I then ask pupils to describe a more sensible approach to this and from there we discuss the importance of balance in their lives. In order to help pupils assess their activities and time commitments, it helps to view their workload on a weekly basis.

Ask pupils to get their timetables out, ideally one which has a full list of their activities as well as classes. If they don't have this, provide them with a copy of the timetable on page 72 to complete. Encourage pupils to add all details of their activities and assess for themselves if they are managing their workload. Have they missed any homework deadlines? Do they feel well? Allow pupils to check in with you one to one to help them reflect on their commitments and encourage them to review things. This can also serve as an opportunity to encourage those who aren't doing enough to consider an activity, study session or commitment.

Discussion

It is important to discuss with pupils the impact of being overcommitted and potentially architects of their own burn out. Homework, extra/co/super curriculums activities are proven to all be effective for pupil's health, wellbeing and academic success, but crucially that is where the balance is correct. As a teacher of health and wellbeing, having discussions with pupils about workload and commitments is part and parcel of teaching them. Again, it stands as an important life lesson to ensure that pupils are taking steps towards ensuring they have the correct balance of activity, commitments and downtime in their lives.

Frequency
This task should be revisited during busy times of the year and in advance of examination diets to ensure pupils are supported.

65 Mental health

Resources: none
Preparation: none

Fortunately, throughout the year we have a number of days specifically dedicated to raising awareness of mental health; children's mental health week is typically commemorated in February and World Mental Health Day in October, see page 85. These points in the calendar are timely reminders for us to discuss these important issues.

In the last set of PISA data, which included the UK, there were inquiries regarding students' life satisfaction and wellbeing. These findings indicated that, on average, British students reported slightly lower life satisfaction levels compared to the OECD average. With rates among our SEND pupils being lower than the average. Additionally, reports such as the Royal College of Paediatrics and Child Health's 'State of Child Health 2020' have shown that, worryingly, progress in children's health and wellbeing in the UK has not only stagnated but has reversed. So it is important to discuss the challenges facing young people and normalise the need for discussion and solutions.

 Instructions
Let pupils know that mental health is as important as physical health and that it is a normal aspect of everyone. Use relatable examples to explain that just as we all have good days and bad days physically, we also have times when we feel happy, sad, anxious or stressed. This normalises that life comprises ups and downs.

Encourage an open dialogue by sharing that it is perfectly okay to feel a range of emotions and that seeking help when things are tough is a positive step. Use inclusive language, such as 'we all' or 'everyone' to emphasise that no one is alone in experiencing these feelings.

Introduce simple, age-appropriate terms to describe different emotions and mental health conditions, and explain that it is okay to talk about how we feel. You might say 'Just like we can catch a cold, sometimes our minds need some care and attention too', and this highlights that sometimes if we feel down more often than we don't, and if this makes it hard for us to complete our everyday activities, then it is time to seek help.

Reinforce the idea that seeking help is a sign of strength. Discuss the various forms of support available, such as talking to friends, family, teachers or school counsellors, and using professional resources like Childline. Remind pupils that taking care of their mental health is just as important as taking care of their physical health.

 Discussion
Mental health and wellbeing belongs on every PSE curriculum and is likely something your pupils will discuss in their guidance groups, so I i's worth liaising with your head of year or guidance teacher to ensure complementary Tutor time.

Frequency
Regularly mentioning mental health and wellbeing will normalise them and help support pupils.

66   To-do/Taa daa lists

Resources: To-do list sheet, pens/pencils
Preparation: 5 Minutes to gather and distribute resources
Feelings of overwhelm can have a big impact on pupils. Following on from the previous points on page 111, pupils need support to manage their workloads. Showing and encouraging time and task management approaches is a super way to help. Effective time and task management significantly supports pupils by providing structure, clarity and control over daily activities.

My own personal way of managing my workload is to create a to-do list. Once everything has been scored off, it becomes my ta-da list! A well-organised to-do list with realistic time allocations and buffer periods ensures tasks are completed without last-minute rushes and tools like to-do lists and planners help track progress, reducing cognitive load. Teaching pupils exactly how to record their tasks and work through them helps support them to become proficient in managing their time and tasks, leading to a greater sense of achievement and hopefully overall reduction in stress levels.

 Instructions
Introduce the theme of time and task management. Acknowledge that most teens have a lot of demands on their time, with the average pupil in the UK

Tutor time for health and wellbeing

Image 4.3 To Do List Template

spending around two hours a week on homework alone. Empathise with the difficulties this can create during busy periods like in the run-up to exams.

Share your best way of managing your own workload – for me this is always using lists but if you have a better way you believe in, then discuss that. If using the to-do list, share with pupils the page below and ask them to have a go filling it out and arranging their task in order of priority by importance and deadline. Encourage pupils to get into positive habits with managing workload by revisiting this on a regular basis and facilitate time in their day for organisation.

Discussion

This task is a skill for life and certainly one I wish I had considered long before I figured it out. With multiple classes, the quantity of homework can build up quickly so it's important to encourage pupils to adopt and practice positive habits. Managing workload by revisiting this on a regular basis and facilitating time in their day for organisation.

Frequency

This activity can be revisited on a regular basis.

67 Grief and responding to world events

Resources: none
Preparation: none

This is a sensitive topic and one often best left to a longer PSE class where pupils have the chance to follow up the session with their guidance teachers. However, as we have seen in recent times, national and world events may force you, the tutor, to address an incident or loss that is significant. The death of a monarch, a national incident, the onset of a pandemic, the passing of a teacher or other similar situations may be ones you find yourself addressing as a tutor teacher and it is not an easy task to find the right words. Responding to this will require sensitivity, tact and self-awareness.

Instruction

1. Acknowledge the incident or situations in a factual way that provides pupils with an outline of the situation. This can be important, for example as COVID-19 became more a pronounced threat within the UK, misinformation resulted in a vast amount of concern and worry for many people.

Tutor time for health and wellbeing

Presenting a factual outline of the situation can help ameliorate the impact of fake news. For example, if you were addressing a class following the death of a monarch, do not shy away from saying clearly that this person has died. Terms such as 'passed away' while more gentle can be less clear for pupils. If you have details, let them know of any future events, or

2. Identify that it is OK to feel a range of emotions, or indeed a vacuum of emotions. In sad or uncertain times there is no one best way to feel. Give pupils permission to feel what they feel, even if they have no direct link to the incidents or situation.
3. Reflect on the thoughts and range of emotions and consider using the strategy on page 104 to encourage pupils to assess how they are.
4. Encourage pupils to be kind to themselves.
5. Reassure pupils of where they can go and who can help them if they need it.

 Discussion

In the course of being a tutor it is inevitable that you will end up having to guide pupils through a vast array of situations. There is rarely an instruction manual for these often-unique circumstances but it is best to be guided by wider principles. You are there to help pupils make sense of the world and life. Your ability to manage this and help pupils hinges on your own wellbeing and self-regulation too. Take care of yourself and remember that as a tutor teacher you are not alone in dealing with challenging situations but should be able to call upon the support of guidance staff, year heads of year and others.

 Frequency

As necessary.

SLEEP

Below is a brief outline explaining a little about sleep and it should be enough to arm the tutor with the knowledge and insight to revisit this vital topic in casual conversation and in a more structured method to introduce sleep diaries and approaches to sleep hygiene.

Sleep has its own subsection but it is of vital importance for our young people, for learners and all humans who want to think well, be well and feel well. I cannot stress enough how foundational it is for our pupils to have adequate sleep and the knowledge of where to get help and who to turn to if they are struggling,

One of the central human needs is sleep. Sleep is profoundly vital at all life stages, affecting mental, physical and emotional health as well as cognitive abilities. Simply put, without adequate sleep, our pupils will struggle. It is estimated that up to 90% of teens do not routinely get enough sleep (Pearson, Sherar and Hamer, 2019). Just as hunger signals our need to eat, our internal feelings of tiredness or exhaustion signal our need for rest and sleep. I strongly believe that we teachers have an important role in educating young people about the importance of getting adequate sleep and how to do it. Below is a brief outline explaining a little about sleep and it should be enough to arm the tutor with the knowledge and insight to revisit this vital topic in casual conversation and in a more structured method to introduce sleep diaries and approaches to sleep hygiene.

The sheer volume of research identifying sleep as a foundational need that underpins much of what we aim to achieve in education influenced my decision to detail sleep needs, strategies and information. I know two things to be true: sleep is essential for successful learning, and teens generally do not get enough of it.

Yet, I have had many conversations with busy, often overwhelmed teenagers who present well-articulated arguments that essentially amount to one thing: they are too busy to sleep. School work, social lives, sports, gaming, and family time must fit into the limited hours outside school and sleep. This overwhelming schedule can contribute to their lack of sleep. It is hard to argue that our need for sleep is not inconvenient. In evolutionary terms, needing to disconnect from our environment for nearly a third of the day is quite inconvenient!

Tononi and Cirelli (2003), along with many others, have conducted compelling research detailing the rich and complex activities facilitated by sleep. During the day, learning and experiences are so abundant that they need to be reorganised and strengthened, leading to growth in the brain's structure and functional abilities. Night-time brain activities support this process. Cognitive impairment resulting from sleep deprivation supports this theory, highlighting that sleep is essential for neural reorganisation and the growth of the brain's structure and function. During infancy, childhood and adolescence, learning and development are more pronounced than in adult years, which is suggested as the reason why young people require longer periods of rest.

Sleep is an active and vital process during which the brain operates differently than during wakefulness. It engages various brain regions and neural pathways responsible for memory formation, waste clearance and overall brain health. The brain's glymphatic system, which is activated during sleep, removes waste products like beta-amyloid. Increased beta-amyloid levels, associated with sleep deprivation, are thought to play a key role in the development of Alzheimer's disease.

Sleep significantly impacts learning and memory retention by allowing the brain to consolidate and process information from daily experiences. It strengthens neural connections formed during wakefulness, crucial for memory consolidation. Research shows that individuals who sleep after learning new information recall it better than those who do not. Slow wave sleep (SWS), or deep sleep, is particularly important for memory consolidation as it involves the transfer of information from short-term to long-term memory. Sleep also supports neuroplasticity, enabling the brain to adapt to new experiences and integrate new information.

Lack of sleep negatively affects young people, potentially leading to poor academic performance, attention and memory issues, and increased accident risk due to impaired reaction time and decision-making abilities. Sleep deprivation can also cause mood swings and irritability, exacerbated by hormonal changes in adolescence. Furthermore, adequate sleep is essential for physical health, supporting a strong immune system and regulating hunger and metabolism. Teenagers are especially vulnerable to sleep deprivation as their bodies undergo significant growth and change during this period.

The sleep needs of pupils are often addressed in the personal, social and health education (PSHE) curriculum for various year groups, and rightly so. These curriculums are designed to support pupils throughout their school years and prepare them for life afterward. Given the nature of secondary school timetabling, these sessions often become weekly events. My decision to include this suggestion stems from the belief that addressing sleep issues is an ongoing process, not a one-off lesson, and every class teacher can contribute to promoting healthy sleep habits.

68 Sleep diary

Resources: sleep diary, pens/pencils
Preparation: five minutes to gather and distribute resources
The first tutor activity relating to sleep is to encourage pupils to think about their own sleep habits through keeping a sleep diary. This activity may be timed to complement similar discussions in PSE classes where self-care and physiological needs are likely to be topics of discussion. Sleep is such a central need for young people and getting enough can be a challenge. Do not worry about replication, or overkill, in delivering this session.

Transforming Your Tutor Time Curriculum

WEEKLY SLEEP DIARY

Day	What activities did you do after 5pm (Sport, TV, Homework etc)	Bedtime	Wake-up Time	Total Hours of Sleep	How rested did you feel the next morning 1-----5	Notes
Sunday	• Football training until 8pm • 30 mins of phone time	10.00 PM	6:30 AM	8.5		Woke up once during the night
Monday						
Tuesday						
Wednesday						
Thursday						

Image 4.4 Sleep Diary Template

Copyright material from Kirsten Colquhoun (2025), Transforming Your Tutor Time Curriculum, Routledge.

Tutor time for health and wellbeing

It is also worth considering the timing of this activity for exams, or other typically challenging times for pupils as they may find it more important to think about their self-care during pressured times, like exams. Visiting this topic regularly in a low stakes way will hopefully support pupils in building positive habits. The completion of a weekly sleep diary is an excellent place to start and will hopefully encourage pupils to reflect on their sleep habits.

Instructions
Issue pupils at the start of the week with either a paper copy, or if you are confident everyone has access to a device, a digital version of this. Discuss the different sections with pupils and ask them to consider what an ideal bedtime routine looks like for them. Share with them that around 90% of teens do not get enough sleep and use the information on page 117 to highlight the importance of adequate sleep for their wellbeing, health and learning. Pupils should be able to fill in the first row of the table. Then revisit each morning of the week and provide time for pupils to add in their details.

Discussion
At the end of week pupils reflect on their sleep habits and consider which nights were better than others. Encourage pupils to draw conclusions about their sleep routines and to consider making two aims to improve their sleep. Some of the next activities might be considered depending on your timings for tutor time. This task is also worth revisiting throughout the year to see how things are progressing.

Frequency
Visiting this a couple of times a year so pupils are prompted to observe any changes themselves and have an opportunity to seek help is a good idea.

69 Sleep needs

Resources: completed sleep diary, pens/pencils, internet and projector
Preparation: five minutes to gather and distribute resources
To fully understand the sleep diary and draw meaningful conclusions from it, pupils need to recognise the importance of sleep for their bodies and minds. Using tutor time to remind pupils of this essential physiological need is an excellent way to integrate this foundational topic into regular discussions. As discussed on page 117, the importance of sleep cannot be underestimated, and

therefore it should be championed as a topic of discussion whenever possible. The key here is to have gentle coaching conversations with pupils and enable them to link their actions and outcomes as well as plan for improvement.

 Instructions

- Using the data collected on the sheet, ask pupils to work out their average numbers of hours of sleep each night.
- Share with pupils the recommendations for teenagers and sleep, the following websites are reliable sources:
  - www.hopkinsmedicine.org/health/wellness-and-prevention/teenagers-and-sleep-how-much-sleep-is-enough
  - www.nationwidechildrens.org/specialties/sleep-disorder-center/sleep-in-adolescents
  - www.bupa.co.uk/newsroom/ourviews/sleep-patterns-in-teenagers
- Encourage pupils to reflect on their approaches to sleep and start to plan for improvement with two clear goals for now.

 Discussion

Depending on the extent of pupils' findings there may be a need for targeted support here. As discussed on page 38 the key to effective health promotion in schools is to ensure it is woven within the fabric of what we do, and not treated like an added extra, bolted on at the end of the lesson or day. Setting aside time and placing the emphasis on pupil interpretation creates the perfect environment for self-reflection and ownership of the issues.

 Frequency

This session is a good follow up to the previous one and should be done in tandem with it

70 Sleep hygiene – How to get more sleep

Resources: paper, pens/pencils or notebook for pupils to record their plans
Preparation: five minutes to gather and distribute resources
Highlighting the need for sleep is just one part of the approach to helping young people prioritise this central psychological need. Providing pupils with practical guidance and help to improve their sleep habits is a good use of tutor time.

Instructions

Establishing the importance of sleep will hopefully help pupils understand the significance of this session and encourage them to listen.

Share the following guidance with young people, this can be done in preparation for the sleep diary, or following the sleep diary to support improvements

1. Encourage pupils to maintain a consistent sleep timetable

    Hard as it might be, having a regular bedtime and wake time even on weekends is a key way to promote good sleep. Go to bed and wake up at the same time every day, including weekends. Encourage pupils to limit daytime naps to 20–30 minutes and avoid napping late in the afternoon.

2. Suggest creating a relaxing pre sleep routine (or at least minimise stressful discussions and activities in the hour before bed, this includes homework!)

    Suggest pupils consider calming activities such as reading, taking a warm bath or practising relaxation exercises. This means limiting screen time for at least an hour before bed, as blue light can interfere with melatonin production (some recent research indicates that the impact of blue light may have been overly exaggerated, however the stimulation of devices still makes them work before bed). You might want to guide them towards writing this down or making a specific plan.

3. Improve your sleep environment

    Advise pupils to ensure their mattress and pillows are comfortable and supportive. Keep the bedroom cool, use blackout curtains and minimise noise with earplugs or white noise machines if necessary and keep the bedroom tidy to create a more restful environment!

4. Mind your diet and exercise

    Recommend that pupils avoid caffeine, energy drinks and nicotine as these stimulants can disrupt sleep patterns, so avoid them, especially in the afternoon and evening. This might encourage a wider discussion about stimulants and their impacts.

5. Exposure to natural light

    Share with pupils that getting outside once they wake up is essential for helping set their biological needs for sleep. Spending time outside in the morning to help regulate their sleep-wake cycle is a hugely effective way of helping with sleep. Discuss ways of building this into busy routines. Could tutor time be taken outside perhaps?

Make sure to signpost the places pupils can find out more about healthy sleep hygiene and where they can turn to for help if sleep becomes troublesome for them.

Discussion
Prompting discussion and reflection of current habits while highlighting some good approaches is enough to start the conversation off. Ideally, revisiting the lessons on sleep, in line with a Dave Brailsford approach (see page 36), is enough to support improvements. Drip feeding adjustments to habits rather than expecting or promoting dramatic shifts and changes is more likely to create sustained and manageable improvement overtime.

Discussing this with pupils as a whole rather than enabling them to wear sleep deprivation like a badge of honour is perhaps the more favourable of approaches.

Frequency
Again, this session will work well on a biannual basis or in response to any issues or concerns you have with your tutor group.

71 Healthy bodies/physical health

Resources: none
Preparation: none
Promoting physical fitness is crucial for our pupils' overall health wellbeing. Regular physical activity helps improve cardiovascular health, strengthens muscles and bones and boosts mental health by reducing stress and anxiety. It can act as a positive means to make friends and connect with others. Encouraging our students to be active sets them on a path towards a healthier lifestyle, which can also positively impact their academic performance and concentration. But it can also be one of the first things to go when pupils start to feel overwhelmed by schoolwork so it is vital we use tutor time to reflect and encourage.

Instructions
Start by introducing the concept of physical health in an age- and stage-appropriate and relatable way. For example, *Physical health means taking care of our bodies so they stay strong and work well. Just like how we need to charge our phones to keep them running, our bodies need certain things to stay healthy and full of energy.*

Explain the benefits of physical health clearly, highlighting both the immediate and long-term advantages. Depending on the age and stage of your group you can be as detailed or as brief as required. For example, *being physically active helps us in many ways.*

1. It makes our hearts stronger, helps us build muscles and bones, and can even improve our mood. When we exercise, our brains release chemicals that make us feel happier and less stressed. Staying active can also help us concentrate better in class and learn more effectively.
2. To make the concept more engaging, explain to pupils the impact physical activity can have on our brains. Discussing some of the following may interest pupils:

    During physical activity, especially aerobic exercise, the body releases endorphins. These are chemicals produced by the central nervous system and the pituitary gland that act as natural painkillers. They not only help to alleviate pain but also promote a sense of wellbeing and even euphoria!

    Not only that but exercise also increases the production and release of neurotransmitters such as serotonin, dopamine and noradrenaline. These chemicals are fundamental for mood regulation, and their elevated levels can lead to improved mood, greater feelings of pleasure and a reduction in anxiety and stress.

    Last, physical activity helps to lower levels of stress hormones, such as cortisol. Lowering these hormones can contribute to a calmer state of mind, helping individuals feel more relaxed and less anxious after exercising. This is especially important during the run-up to exams.

You may wish to provide pupils with articles or links to learn more about how exercise impacts the brain, body and mind. Or invite pupils to share their favourite activities and how this makes them feel during and afterwards. Here I like to share my own experiences of not always feeling like going to the gym but always feeling better and glad I did and how exercise can be destressing and energising.

Discussion

This session may become more important before exams and mock exams. Reminding pupils to look after their body as well as their mind is essential for their overall wellbeing. Encourage pupils to think about the reasons why maintaining physical health is important. It is also worth raising this early on with pupils as we encourage them to engage with extra/co/super curriculums activities.

Invite pupils to share their thoughts and experiences with physical activity and encourage them to set personal goals for staying active to keep the conversation going and share in their successes too.

 Frequency

Alongside the discussion about extra and co-curricular activities there are ways to weave this into discussion regularly.

72 Sign posting help

Resources: none
Preparation: none

This session works well as a follow-on from the one on mental health on page 104. It is vital to ensure our pupils know where to turn if they are having a tough time and the best time to share this is before they need it. Using tutor time to help prepare pupils for the ups and downs of life is an excellent use of these sessions. Arm pupils with the knowledge of where to turn through encouraging them to seek support from trusted adults in their lives, whether it is parents, guardians or teachers can make a significant difference. Additionally, organisations like Childline offer a safe space for children to talk about their concerns confidentially.

 Instructions

Begin by discussing the importance of seeking help when facing difficulties, explore some of times when we all need a little more support and try to use positive language to destigmatise and normalise the ups and downs we can all feel in response to life events and situations. Doing this should help create a supportive atmosphere where pupils feel comfortable talking about their feelings and challenges.

Encourage pupils to think about trusted adults in their lives, such as family members, teachers or school guidance staff and even yourself. Highlight the role of these adults in providing guidance and support. Inform pupils about professional resources like Childline, explaining what they offer and how pupils can contact them. Provide clear instructions on how to access these services.

Tutor time for health and wellbeing

Discussion
You will not be alone in this endeavour and it might be worth checking in with the year head or pastoral support staff to share your intentions of doing this session if it can be timed to complement other efforts. Ensure that the contact details for support services are easily accessible to pupils. This can be done by displaying posters in classrooms, providing leaflets or adding the information to the school's website or student handbook. Regularly remind pupils about these resources and encourage them to use them whenever necessary. Reinforce the message that seeking help is a sign of strength, not weakness.

Frequency
This session might work as a good, targeted sessions in response to concerns or issues.

73 Feedback for safe/healthy/achieving and whole school improvement QA

Resources: Online survey provider, the internet
Preparation: time to write the survey

Incorporating pupil feedback and allowing them to reflect on their school experiences is crucial for fostering an inclusive and supportive learning environment. OFSTED, HMIE and UNESCO emphasise the importance of involving young people in decision-making processes. Providing opportunities for pupil voice and choice, allowing them to participate in decision-making, and giving them a say in their own learning processes can significantly enhance their sense of connection to the school, thereby improving their overall wellbeing. Article 12 of the United Nations Convention on the Rights of the Child (UNCRC) states that children and young people should have a say in decisions affecting their lives.

Instructions
One effective method for gathering pupil feedback is through the use of online surveys. By asking pupils to rate their experiences in different aspects of school on a 1–5 scale, the data collected becomes clear and easily interpretable. In terms of the actual questions asked, this should come from either situations you are aware of in school causing tensions (for example creating a survey to ask pupils which types of clubs and societies they are interested in attending is a

good way to match supply and demand), or asking pupils how they feel about tutor time activities and what is missing is a useful tool to ensure pupils are being given a chance to have their say. There is, of course, no expectation that we change everything on a whim, but pupil voices are part of the jigsaw and it is important to make time and space to establish what it looks like.

Using questions which provide quantitative data will ensure that this does not become an overly burdensome task. This quantifiable data can then be shared with pupils, allowing them to see the impact of their feedback and understand how their input is being used to shape their school environment.

 Discussion

There are two primary benefits to this, first, it models the democratic process for them, which is essential for an orderly and effective community in various aspects of family, work and political life that our young people will engage with at some level. Second, when pupils feel included and respected and understand the rationale behind decisions, it is much more likely that there will be harmony when implementing changes. Englund, Graham and Dinsmore (2003) noted that 'understanding the motives and logic for change of the leaders helps create better participants and followers'. This engagement can also involve retrospectively asking pupils for feedback on how something is working out.

 Frequency

This session will work well on an annual basis and can help feed into planning for future years' tutor time curriculum,

74 Gratitude

Resources: paper, pens/pencils
Preparation: five minutes to gather and distribute resources

Supporting the practice of pupils writing down their gratitudes is a powerful tool to support their wider wellbeing. Encouraging pupils to regularly reflect on and express gratitude has been shown to have numerous positive effects on mental and emotional health and like the sessions on hope and hopefulness can promote positive habits for life, and can enhance their overall happiness and resilience, enabling them to better cope with challenges and setbacks.

Tutor time for health and wellbeing

 Instructions
Facilitating gratitude exercises can be straightforward and impactful. Allocate a few minutes each day or week for pupils to jot down a few things they are grateful for in a private, personal manner. Encourage them to be specific and reflect on both significant and everyday moments of gratitude.

1. Begin by explaining to pupils what gratitude is and why it is important. Discuss how focusing on the positive aspects of their lives can improve their mood, relationships and overall wellbeing. Provide examples of things they might feel grateful for, such as a kind friend, a helpful teacher, a fun activity or even something as simple as a sunny day. Focus on small actions, this is not an exercise in appreciating their new smartphone, or fancy trainers!
2. Provide pupils with journals, notebooks or gratitude cards where they can record their thoughts. Encourage them to write down at least three things they are grateful for, being as specific as possible. Remind them that there is no reason to share or feel pressured to show anyone else.
3. If you are comfortable, reflect on the fact that you are grateful for and model how important it is to take time to actively find the positives in your life.

 Discussion
Practising gratitude can have both a short- and long-term impact on our schools and individual pupils. Our cognitive design means we are often more predisposed to remember highly emotional events and these, for teens, can lead to negative cycles of thoughts. When pupils are guided to acknowledge the kindness and support they receive from peers and teachers, it can strengthen their sense of belonging and connection. This, in turn, can lead to a more supportive and cohesive school environment in the immediate and long term.

 Frequency
This activity can be revisited annually or termly.

75 Managing digital distractions

Resources: none
Preparation: none
Most of us are on screens more now than ever before. This is not always a bad thing unless they are sapping our time and focusing away from the task

at hand. We know from talking to young people themselves that screen time can often be distracting. Twenge and Campbell's (2018) research indicates that more hours of screen time is associated with lower wellbeing in ages 2 to 17; high users show less curiosity, self-control and emotional stability. Associations with wellbeing were greater for adolescents than for children.

It is important to note, especially in conversation with young people, that not all screen time is bad and that there are many benefits that come from having access to the online world, especially when time is spent purposefully. Our focus here is not so much about time spent online, but in helping pupils work out how to guard their screen free home, revision or downtime, and keeping it safe from the lure and distractions phones, tablets and other technology is expertly designed to exploit. Discussion should centre on informing pupils of the cost of distraction both to their focus and the quality of their learning. Draw awareness to the challenges that come with managing digital distractions and the potential costs of not doing this. A person's brain has to work much harder to get back into a task if distracted. This has an impact on both the efforts required, energy expended and of course the quality of the learning.

 Instructions

Open up discussion about the distractions and challenges often incurred when completing homework and revision. Allow pupils to chat this through in small groups. This helps pupils to identify their challenges without demonising technology, as doing so might make the conversation a much harder one. Instead, the focus should be on understanding how to manage these distractions effectively.

Encourage pupils to pinpoint their specific distractions, whether it is their phone, social media, watch notifications, group chats or other forms of entertainment. Share details about the falsehoods of multitasking and the realities of cost-switching. That is the brain power required when we switch between tasks rather than *mono-task* with one thing. The consequence of multitasking is fatigue which impacts the quality of learning and ability to process and retain information.

Next, encourage pupils to consider some approaches to minimising and managing these distractions. Ask pupils to consider setting boundaries as a practical approach, for example using apps to block notifications for a specific period of time or aiming for a technology-free hour once a day, and keeping phones on silent and out of sight during study sessions. It is also beneficial to turn off notifications altogether, as even a glimpse of the phone can be a distraction! Building on previous sessions, ask pupils how they could make small, manageable changes that leverage the impact of marginal gains and help form sustainable habits. It is always helpful to encourage pupils to enlist the support of family and carers when studying and ask for help to minimise the distraction incurred by phones and other technology.

Last, discuss how ring-fencing time for digital activities, gaming, communicating or researching can be a positive and healthy part of anyone's routine and you are by no means seeking to end their online enjoyment.

Discussion

Pupils will benefit from revising this session throughout the year and being prompted to consider the improvements they have made and assess if it has been effective. Phones, tablets and screens are masterfully designed to elicit our attention and it is no surprise that they do so with ease! Keep the conversation ongoing and be open to coaching pupils little and often, there are no silver bullets coming to help manage the screen time in all our lives. Managing time effectively will help overall wellbeing and support pupils in managing their workload, but more than that this is a life skill that is of greater importance now as we move further into our digital journey.

Frequency

Again, this session is an excellent proactive and reactive one that can be delivered as and when you, the form tutor, know it is needed.

Part V
Tutor time for academic improvement

At the heart of every school is a desire and aim to provide an excellent education for the young people who attend. Teachers, leaders and school staff tirelessly search for means and ways to ensure pupils have the chance to learn and flourish during their years in secondary education, setting pupils up for their next steps.

Yet, time and again, when I speak with pupils about their challenges, I hear back that there are two main things they find hard about the learning they do. The first is coping with the demands on them during exam time. This feedback does not come as a surprise and is echoed in research findings including the work by Cosmas et al. (2020) which suggests that there is a small yet consistent decline in mental wellbeing as school work pressure increases, and this is especially present in high-income countries, and correlations evident in the PISA data. Björn Högberg's 2021 work suggests that the increasing stress pupils feel surrounding schools is due to the increased pressures on them to gain excellent results. The demand for which is often driven by economic change and educational pressure, coupled with increased availability of distractions like screens and tech, we have the perfect storm for pupil mental health. It is important to recognise that these drivers are not changing or diminishing. We therefore have to consider the approaches we take to supporting pupils who understandably find this element of school life challenging and support them to build a toolkit of proven study techniques. Utilising tutor time is a key way of doing this as a whole-school intervention, and one that can easily be monitored and assessed for impact.

Exam pressures alone are not the sole cause of pupils experiencing difficulty with self-directed revision, other factors include neurobiological factors like executive function development, and personal factors including relationships and the environment a young person is in all impact their mental health. Earlier sections in this book have details to support you, the tutor, in helping your pupils to build positive relationships both with themselves and their peers and build positive lifestyle habits. This section aims to support you to arm pupils with excellent methods for learning. As teachers, we have huge power to positively impact our pupils' academic preparedness for school, exams and beyond. The following section considers research-informed approaches that can help pupils in their learning, revision and consolidation and drive whole-school success.

The second thing pupils – in abundance – have told me they find challenging about schools is finding effective revision techniques. Over the years many pupils have told me that in absence of understanding *what* to do, they tend to fall back on either rewriting their class notes or rereading them, highlighting material and spending time doing what we know to be less effective means of revision. The meta-analysis by Dunlosky et al. (2013) of over 400 research papers offers valuable insights that can support us in directing pupils with this. The study reviewed hundreds of research papers to evaluate ten popular techniques, rating each one based on how well it supports long-term learning. Interestingly, some of the methods that pupils commonly use are among the least effective, while other lesser utilised approaches are more effective.

Within the paper, two techniques emerged as particularly effective across different subjects, ages and contexts. First, practice testing which involves actively recalling information through methods like flashcards or self-testing was found to be highly beneficial. This approach strengthens memory by requiring pupils to actively retrieve information rather than passively recognise it, and it has proven effective across a wide range of topics and learning levels. The second high-impact strategy is distributed practice and spacing. By breaking study sessions into chunks over time rather than cramming, pupils can boost retention considerably, as spaced learning helps move information into long-term memory for easier recall when they need it most.

The paper found strategies with moderate impact, which can be helpful but might not be as consistent depending on the context. Elaborative interrogation, for instance, involves asking 'why' questions to explore reasons behind concepts, helping pupils connect new material with their existing knowledge, and therefore building their schema. Self-explanation, where pupils explain how new information relates to what they know or walk through steps while solving problems, can improve understanding and build confidence. Interleaved practice, mixing different types of problems or topics within a study session, was found to be especially useful in subjects like maths, where it helps pupils develop adaptability in problem-solving.

It is worth noting that many of the most popular strategies among pupils, including highlighting, rereading and summarising notes, were shown to have limited impact on longer term retention and understanding. As educators, we know that these approaches to revision are much less effective than retrieval practices. These passive methods do not require as much thinking and so do not encourage active engagement, making them less effective for long-term learning.

These insights remind us that we can support our pupils by encouraging them to adopt high-impact techniques like practice testing and spaced learning, both of which have been shown to consistently improve outcomes. While some familiar strategies might feel natural, it is often the active, retrieval-focused methods that make the biggest difference. By incorporating small lessons on how to apply these strategies into tutor time, we can help pupils make the most of their study time and build habits that genuinely support their success at school and after.

Karpicke and Blunt's (2011) research clearly demonstrates the significant gains pupils make when they approach revision in a systematic way. Tutor time is an ideal opportunity for supporting our pupils and reinforcing positive study habits, reviewing their progress and learning more about how to help themselves in school outside of specific subjects. This, for many tutors, may feel like a more natural extension of their regular role in the classroom as visiting the tools, methods and approaches to support excellent learning is something many teachers will do as part of their subject delivery.

Hopefully undertaking this in a 'neutral' territory helps pupils apply their knowledge of study skills across all of their subjects and empowers pupils with universal approaches to revision and studying in helping them at school and afterwards. This also creates a 'catch all' opportunity which ensures all pupils are given this vital information and not just those whose teachers explicitly discuss revision strategies. For whole-school improvements this is a vital approach. Taking stock, reflecting on the current situation and then planning for changes is a life skill and something you can support for great outcomes.

It really helps to share the details of how knowledge is created with pupils so they can clearly see the reasoning behind the likes of dual coding, retrieval practice, interleaving and so on. Sharing details of how learning happens in the brain can demonstrate to pupils that there are key factors and inputs they can activate for success.

Tutors in a school will comprise a vast array of subject specialists well placed to support young people in acquiring the academic skill to thrive in all areas of the curriculum. Using tutor time to support our learning is an excellent opportunity to support our pupils' overall success which underpins positive wellbeing.

There are a number of ways tutors can do this. Using tutor time to explore effective revision activities and ensure pupils have the knowledge and skills of *how* to learn can support the academic progress of pupils.

Using tutor time to support interventions is a popular approach, especially in the post-lockdown era. I spoke with one Trust who used a fair chunk of tutor time for guided reading to help increase the literacy standard of their young people. This decision was made following a data-informed discussion where it was clear that the academic standards being achieved in English needed wider support than could be provided within the allocated time for this class. In this instance pupils were provided with explicit instructions, pages and questions and were guided to read and begin analysing texts. The chosen texts were different to the ones being used in English class, but the questions and analytical skills were deeply tied to the academic standards. Again we see tutor time being used to support wider improvement like those discussed on page 136 and this of course is an excellent use of it. One thing to be mindful of here is that within this approach we need to be wary not to confuse familiarity and rehearsal with competence and learning. Group approaches to guided reading have their place but without feedback, challenge and support they can mask individual issues. Again, it is important to be guided by the data and review of all interventions to ensure their impact.

I spoke to other schools who, amid the SEN/D crisis, were reallocating tutor time to enable pupils with EHCPs to obtain specific support with different specialists. This is an increasingly common approach and while it has the ability to maximise the capacity we have in a timetable we must be careful not to view SEN/D provision as something that can be slotted in. In the next section I discuss approaches tutors can take to support all pupils and especially those with SEN/D needs.

The next section of this book is split into the three ways we can utilise this time to effectively enhance academic capabilities:

1. **Academic interventions**

    Incorporating short literacy, numeracy and SEN/D focused activities can greatly benefit students' reading and writing skills. This could include

reading a short passage together, vocabulary building, organisation workshops or quick writing prompts.
2. **Revision planning**
Guiding pupils to prepare for effective revision is an important part of school life. Effective target setting, review of resources and timetable planning are useful things to explore to support pupils.
3. **Strategies in action**
Teaching explicit strategies for revisions is time well spent, from effective retrieval practice, where they recall previously learned material, to the more effective way to use flashcards can enhance long-term retention and understanding.

The beauty of these activities lies in their cumulative impact. By using this time wisely, we not only help pupils master essential skills and knowledge but also build their competences and confidence for learning. This, in turn, feeds into their wider motivations and overall wellbeing, creating a positive cycle of competence, success, and wellbeing.

Sub-section 1: Academic interventions

Linking directly to your whole-school improvement plan, these activities are designed to be low-stakes opportunities to reinforce and improve pupils' core skills. Ideally, subject-specific expertise should be accessed prior to planning this element of the tutor time Curriculum as this will ensure pupils can link their experiences here to their wider progress and thus feel a better sense of connection between these two elements of school life.

Ensure that in all of these activities you are providing verbal and written prompts to ensure they are as accessible as possible for everyone in the room and keep the pressure off through the use of whiteboards (pupils can therefore see other answers to check theirs before sharing).

76   Reading programmes

Resources: books
Preparation: five minutes to gather and distribute resources
Increasingly schools are using tutor time to promote literacy and stage literacy interventions. Reading articles, the news or even a class novel

Tutor time for academic improvement

together is a valuable use of time as it supports pupils' literacy skills. When pupils engage with a shared text and subsequent discussion it gives them an opportunity to develop their reading comprehension through discussions and collective analysis. Research suggests that reading fiction might give us an opportunity to experiment with different identities in safe, imagined environments (Slater et al., 2014). Independent reading at school is a topic of debate with critics suggesting that any element of control here can be demotivating for young people. The meta-analysis by Bus, Shang and Roskos (2024) of over 40 studies shows a modesty positive impact for reading motivation and word recognition can emerge through independent reading approaches. However there is no effect of comprehension, suggesting that group reading and discussion should be considered if that is the aim. So it is important to be really clear on your goals if this intervention is being used by you. With any intervention approach, it is important to create a method of measure so you know if it is working.

 Instructions
How you set this up in tutor time will depend on a host of factors from the space in which you take your classes to the size of the class and, depending on the school approach, you may have whole sets of novels available, or you may be responsible for sourcing articles yourself. Making contact with the English department can be a good move to find out if they have any class sets of books available too.

Where feasible, include an element of choice for pupils in the texts you read and critically discuss. Avoid asking pupils to read unless they specifically volunteer. This activity should primarily be to help pupils read for enjoyment, not an additional academic task.

 Discussion
This shared experience encourages them to think deeply about themes, characters and the author's intentions, fostering critical thinking. Additionally, reading aloud together helps improve vocabulary, fluency and expression, making it an enriching and enjoyable way to build essential literacy skills in a supportive, collaborative environment. It helps them 'see the story', thereby enhancing understanding of character thoughts, motivations and action, skills of explanation and

prediction plus alternative directions or endings – they can better visualise the narrative which aids their own writing skills, both fiction and non-fiction.

 Frequency
Depending on your school and pupil needs this could be part of your weekly routine.

77-81 Spelling rules

Building on reading programmes, it is wise to consider setting some time aside to review and revisit common spelling rules that pupils will have certainly been exposed to regularly during their primary years when spelling was a more central focus of their literacy education. Ideally, your school should have a bank of keywords for each subject that can be widely accessed to ensure that the sessions are tied to the academic curriculum and therefore feel more meaningful to pupils. Failing that, liaising with departments and the head of English could be useful to ensure you can pinpoint and focus on commonly misspelt words and common grammatical errors. Other useful and, dare I say, fun activities can include:

77 Spelling word race

Resources: paper, pens/pencils or mini whiteboards
Preparation: five minutes to gather and distribute resources
Choose a list of commonly misspelt or subject-specific words. Pupils can race to write each word correctly on mini whiteboards or in their notebooks, with a focus on accuracy and speed.

78 Crosswords

Resources: blank crosswords or squared paper, pens/pencils
Preparation: five minutes to gather and distribute resources
Using the words from the activity above provide pupils with blank crosswords and instructions to make one up for their partner. Or alternatively tackle one online together as a class.

79 Word building challenge

Resources: paper, pens/pencils or mini whiteboards
Preparation: five minutes to gather and distribute resources
Give pupils a root word and challenge them to create as many related words as possible by adding prefixes and suffixes, for example spell could become misspell, spelling, spelled and so on. This builds their understanding of word structure and helps reinforce correct spellings, and you can add a time challenge in and make it a game.

80 Spot the mistakes

Resources: computer and projector
Preparation: five minutes to write the passage, mini whiteboards
Provide a short passage with deliberate spelling errors. Pupils can work individually or in pairs to identify and correct the mistakes, focusing on words they commonly misspell.

81 Anagram challenge

Resources: computer and projector
Preparation: five minutes to source the anagrams online or make them up, mini whiteboards
Provide pupils with jumbled letters of a word and challenge them to unscramble them. This can be linked to subject-specific vocabulary or tricky spelling words.

Ensure that in all of these activities you are providing verbal and written prompts to ensure they are as accessible as possible for everyone in the room and keep the pressure off through the use of whiteboards (pupils can therefore see other answers to check theirs before sharing).

Frequency
These tasks can be carried out as regularly as you feel appropriate. If there is a whole-school focus on spelling, or literacy, they will help to reinforce this and can be adapted to support these goals.

Numeracy Interventions

Confidence with numeracy is a key indicator of success in secondary schools, but it is also something pupils are highly likely to self-identity as a difficulty they experience. So again, using the Dave Brailsford Approach and visiting some key numeracy skills is a great use of tutor time. If possible, I would advise liaising with the maths department for their input and resources so that there is a coordinated approach to link in usefully with overall aims and objectives. The following activities can prove impactful even with pupils nearing the end of their academic journey. These activities are engaging and focus on reinforcing essential numeracy skills in a short, manageable timeframe.

82 Mental maths

Resources: computer and projector
Preparation: five minutes to source the maths questions online or make them up, mini whiteboards
Set a series of quick questions involving percentages, fractions or ratios. Keep it fast paced and encourage pupils to beat their previous scores to build confidence in mental arithmetic.

83 Times tables

Resources: computer and projector
Preparation: five minutes to source the questions or make them up, mini whiteboards
Even after primary school, times tables are a key skill. Combine straightforward multiplication questions with more complex tasks like finding percentages or fractional parts of numbers.

84 Real-world problem-solving

Resources: Computer and projector
Preparation: five minutes to source the questions or make them up, mini whiteboards
Present real-life scenarios that require maths, such as calculating discounts or splitting costs for events, or speed of travel and time. Pupils can work through the problem in groups to take the pressure off.

85 Number line completion

Resources: number lines, pens/pencils
Preparation: five minutes to gather and distribute resources
Provide number lines with missing values, including decimals or fractions, and ask pupils to fill them in. This builds their understanding of number relationships and spacing and may also be etched in the earlier activities looking into key historical events on timelines.

86 Percentage conversion practice

Resources: mini whiteboards
Preparation: five minutes to prepare the questions, gather and distribute resources
Get pupils to convert between percentages, decimals and fractions. This can be done as a verbal challenge or with quick written responses on mini whiteboards or used in target setting when reflecting on their current successes in different subjects and agreed targets for improvement – get them to work out their marginal gains!

87 Data analysis mini task

Resources: paper, pens/pencils or mini whiteboards
Preparation: time to prepare the task, five minutes to gather and distribute resources
Provide a small data set and ask pupils to calculate key statistics like mean, median or mode. They can also interpret data from simple graphs or tables. If suitable, this might be a good skill to visit in advance of core course work which may require such an approach, again, liaising with class teachers here can only serve to benefit everyone.

88 Daily maths challenge

Resources: paper, pens/pencils or mini whiteboards
Preparation: time to prepare the task, five minutes to gather and distribute resources

Transforming Your Tutor Time Curriculum

Offer a more complex word problem involving percentages, distance or time. Pupils can work through the problem logically, focusing on clear explanations of their reasoning before reviewing the next day. This approach works especially well for days when time might be tight.

89 Countdown TV challenge

Resources: paper, pens/pencils or mini whiteboards
Preparation: time to prepare the task, five minutes to gather and distribute resources

This activity can be seen on Channel 4's popular show 'Countdown'. To start, write a three digit target number on the board and then six smaller numbers – a mix of single and double digits, along with - + x and then with a timer invite pupils to get as close to the number as possible.

 Frequency

These tasks can be carried out as regularly as you feel appropriate. If there is a whole-school focus on numeracy they will help to reinforce this and can be adapted to support these goals.

SEND support

'The system isn't working well for anyone involved: parents, children, teachers, special educational needs schools, and even local councils', declared a former Education Secretary, as she addressed the elephant in the room and confessed the need to improve England's Special Educational Needs and Disabilities (SEND) system.

She was not and is not wrong. The most recent data from the Department for Education underscores the magnitude of the problem. A surge in EHCP requests highlights a system buckling under pressure. Nationally, with only 51% of EHCPs issued on time. Deadlines are not being met, young people and schools are going without the tools to understand and respond to individual needs. And while we wait in hopeful anticipation of that changing, tutor time can offer *some* opportunities to help pupils.

In many cases delays with identification and formalisation of pupil needs and difficulties denies the young person and their teachers' access to the full picture of how to fully support them in education. This has been proven to have a negative impact, with SEN/D pupils being among the most likely to self-exclude and have erratic school attendance.

Tutor time for academic improvement

Solving these enormous issues is not a singular task, or one that can be fixed overnight but one that requires a great deal of time and effort. To meet SEN/D needs sufficiently requires expert approaches, pupil-specific approaches and often time and space to explore via trial and error. Vitally, the young person needs to be included in decision making and discussions of approaches and measures. Adequate staffing and resource allocation is vital but too often is elusive and lacking.

The important thing to remember here is that schools need to consider their approaches more now than ever given that not all pupil needs will be formally identified. Meeting only those who have had the sheer luck of making it through the ever-struggling system and getting a formal diagnosis creates an equity issue, especially as diagnostic deadlines continue to increase.

It is important to be clear, for the sake of both teacher and pupil's wellbeing, **tutor time is *not* the solution here**. There are a host of school systems, approaches and expertise required to even attempt to level up the playing field for a young person with an educational need or disability. What we can do in tutor time is take steps which will be helpful for all pupils, and hopefully especially so for young people whose needs are more complex.

To do this, we have to consider operating in a way that establishes what I call automatic doors. That is, the actions that are helpful for all, and essential for some. For example, establishing routines to support daily organisation checks reinforces positive habits and supports pupils who may have organisational challenges, but importantly, is also beneficial for all pupils. Begin each session by guiding pupils to review their timetables, ensure they have the correct books and materials for the day, and check their planners for homework or upcoming deadlines. This practice reinforces good habits for everyone and helps those with organisational challenges, without treating them differently or making them feel othered. Displaying visual timetables in all classrooms is a really quick win for pupils with dyslexia or who struggle with executive function as they benefit from being able to access the same information in multiple ways. Again this does not only benefit specific pupils; providing and normalising use of visual timetables or colour-coded planners is helpful for supporting everyone in an inclusive and productive way. Previously on page 26 I discussed the need to consider the set-up and organisation of tutor time, from environment to communication.

Use this time to briefly touch base with all pupils which naturally includes those who have additional learning needs, wellbeing needs and other issues going on. Ask open-ended questions about how they're managing their workload, any difficulties they're encountering, and if they need specific support. These check-ins may be carried out by you, or other staff. Asking these questions and facilitating times and space for pupils to reflect and answer not only helps with the day-to-day rituals of organisation, but it also strengthens relations, and builds trust as you become an adult who is consistent and responsive in pupils' lives. This is hugely beneficial for ensuring that bonds are established and pupils will be open to coming to you should they need help with bigger problems and hopefully start to build their connections and contribute to an improved experience of belonging within their school journey. These actions, while small in isolation, are vital links in a long chain of actions that support better outcomes for young people and create a more equitable environment for everyone. Tutor time is a powerful tool in helping transform the day-to-day experiences of young people.

In addition to establishing these automatic doors, tutor time also provides an opportunity for young people to discuss things with the other adults in the school responsible for meeting their needs. Pastoral Leads, Year Heads and SENCOs can use tutor time to catch up with young people without disrupting their academic learning.

Last, merging with the Special Educational Needs Coordinator (SENCO) to identify any emerging needs of pupils in your group and help to support the young person in accessing and understanding the provision in place for them is important. This may involve discussion and preparation for examinations. Be open to these conversations as, again, small actions in tutor time can hugely support pupils for whom examinations pose additional challenges. The following strategies may be worth considering.

90 Routine considerations

Resources: none
Preparation: none
For some pupils simply sticking to their usual routine of checking in with you each day will be enough (and occasionally you may need to do this despite tutor time not being part of their study leave).

91 Typing practise

Resources: computers and typing programmes
Preparation: none
Enabling the young person to log on and practise their typing on the school programmes is also a method of ensuring any additional strategies in place for them are maximised in terms of their effectiveness. This is a great example of a task that can benefit everyone and especially those who need it, without highlighting differences or making anyone feel targeted.

92 Exam considerations

Resources: access to the timetables and information
Preparation: a short amount of time to organise
For some pupils, having the opportunity to visit the room or place they will sit their exams can help them with effective visualisation (as discussed on page 45). All of these small actions can be supported in tutor time to maximise every young person's change of positive outcomes during their school career.

93 Checking timetables

Resources: access to timetables
Preparation: none
Simply prompting pupils with helpful reminders about their exam timetables can also provide an opportunity to maximise their organisation and ensure no one gets the time or dates mixed up!

Many of the strategies above will help all pupils, not only those who have identified needs, so consider approaching these things for everyone and be open and make time for these discussions in tutor time, both as a class and if individuals approach you with questions – you may not be armed with the answers but through this openness the young person has a much greater chance of finding the answers.

 **Frequency**
These tasks can be carried out as regularly as you feel appropriate.

Sub-section 2: Revision planning

The academic activities of school are, like it or not, still measured more often than not in a traditional summative exam. And with this system comes a huge burden and challenge for both teacher and pupils. Often there is a sense of 'training' involved in exam preparation as well as supporting pupils mentally with the challenge of these high-stakes methods. The weighting of the exam depends very much upon the nation and the course being studied but for more pupils, school life will incorporate at least an element of preparation for summative assessment. Certainly, in further education pupils require this and so a part of school must consider how we prepare pupils for this, for school and afterwards.

Unfortunately, we know there are many challenges with using a summative approach to assessment. Here, we will discuss what summative assessment is, how it is used and the difficulties it presents for pupils and schools. Low-achieving pupils frequently experience a drop in self-esteem after summative assessments, whereas there is no such link before the tests. Repeated practice tests (without impactful learning in between) can reinforce poor self-esteem in low achievers. Activities earlier in the book can provide some useful strategies for worried or stressed pupils.

To help offset these challenges, tutor time can be used to guide pupils to shift their focus purely from test performance results to clear, pinpointed learning goals. The section below has been carefully designed to provide opportunities to arm pupils with the methods to help them with the enormous task of revisions exam preparation. Although your specialist subject knowledge is likely to rest in one area of the curriculum, we know that these strategies are universally beneficial and will support pupils in their immediate challenges and as lifelong learners.

94 Revision planning

Resources: course deadlines and course information
Preparation: five minutes to gather and distribute resources
Similar to the guidance earlier in the book on workload planning in order to know what you need to do, you need to know what you need to do! The danger is that pupils can access their online exam or test timetable and the knowledge that this information is a few clicks away can create a false sense

of awareness. Pupils should have printed copies of this to ensure they fully engage with it and are able to share and display a copy of this at home too.

 Instructions

The first task here is to gather all the dates of these forthcoming assessments, deadlines or tests. From there ask pupils to work out the subjects and themes being covered in the test, this will help them collate a useful list of revision areas that can be broken down into specific topics. Now, pupils should have the two central ingredients to start revision planning, the deadlines and the to-do list. The next step is for pupils to consider how competent they are at each topic on this list and this is a key metacognitive skill. Pupils who lack this skill often fall into one of three common traps:

1. focusing on topics they already understand well (often because they enjoy them),
2. spending excessive time on revision (leading to diminishing returns and increased stress),
3. underestimating the time needed for certain topics due to a false sense of confidence.

We can support pupils in developing the skills to access their own competence through providing structure for them to consider. Just like the introduction of a wellbeing scale on page 104, applying a scale to their topic checklist where they rate their understanding on a scale of 0–10 can help them evaluate their knowledge gaps.

From this activity pupils should have a clearer understanding of what areas they need to focus their time on. Advise them to create manageable time blocks with sessions for each topic lasting around 30 minutes. Pupils should build in regular short breaks to avoid burnout – ideally this is when they should access their phones and technology so that it is not interrupting their focused study times!

It is also important to balance their daily routine, revisiting multiple subjects in a day and including a weekly review to reinforce their learning. Research clearly shows that interleaving study topics can significantly enhance learning outcomes for pupils. Taylor and Rohrer (2010) found that students who used interleaved practice scored much higher on tests than those who engaged in blocked practice, even though interleaving might make them feel less confident while learning. Adding to this, Pan and Rickard's (2018) meta-analysis confirmed interleaving, along with spaced practice, substantially improves learning and retention across various subjects. Their findings highlight that interleaving not only aids in recalling different concepts but also helps pupils develop flexibility in their problem-solving skills. Importantly, this highlights the value in adding this to the tutor curriculum, and these universally beneficial strategies can be used in all subjects, ages and stages to help pupils in achieving more effective learning outcomes, and effective use of their time.

Additionally, build flexibility into the plan to account for any unexpected delays, ensuring the timetable remains realistic and focused on steady progress rather than last-minute cramming; pupils should still prioritise their social activities, sports and over extracurricular activities for their overall wellbeing.

Last, use the collated list of topics to create a checklist so they can track their progress by ticking off the list, which can help boost their motivation and keep them on course.

Discussion
Ideally this task should be approached in a number of tutor time sessions and regularly revisited to support pupils in sticking to it. Starting this in the lower secondary years will support pupils to get into good habits and start to get a picture of how to organise themselves when the deadlines start to build up. Revisiting where and who they can get help from in both a practical sense and an emotional one will again support overall wellbeing here. It is also worth discussing when the local libraries are open in case pupils need to build this into their timing too.

Frequency
This session will naturally be more suitable at key points the year as pupils prepare for high-stakes assessments.

95 Habit forming

Resources: none
Preparation: none
Our brains (and especially busy teen brains) are constantly working to conserve energy, which is why many of our actions happen automatically, preventing decision fatigue and overwhelm. While this helps by saving mental resources,

it also makes us vulnerable to developing negative habits that we might not always be in control of. Recently, this topic has gained attention, with many behavioural psychologists and neuroscientists taking their own slant but largely agreeing that habits form through a process called the habit loop.

This loop consists of a prompt, craving, behaviour and reward. For example, when someone sees their phone light up, they engage with it and experience every stage of the loop, this reinforces the habit each time until it becomes automatic. Hence the average smartphone user picks it up around once every 12 minutes (thank goodness many schools have now banned phones!). Understanding this loop is essential for teenagers, as it can help them plan to break negative habits and build positive ones, especially around study routines.

 Instructions

As with all theoretical discussions, the more relatable you can make them to your pupils, the better. So start by drawing their attention to some of the actions they have already undertaken that day, including asking them if they remember tying their shoelaces, picking up their phone this morning, putting toothpaste on then brushing their teeth. If these memories are little less than crystal clear (and hopefully they will be) explain that this is because many of them are automatic, due to the habit loop. Then encourage pupils to identify their own triggers, behaviours and rewards for tying their shoes, putting the toothpaste on, picking up phones and so on.

Then guide them in setting one small, achievable goal to change one habit at a time. Help pupils to identify the loop associated with this habit and create a plan by replacing negative behaviours with positive alternatives. You can link this explicitly to the revision planning above and help pupils create a sensible plan for digital distraction during their 30 minutes of focused work. Finally, emphasise the importance of rewarding themselves for positive changes, as this reinforces the new habit. For example, it could be as simple as giving themselves a ten-minute screen reward for distraction-free revision.

 Discussion

Your aim here is not to drastically change the habits and routines of your pupils but to shed some light and understanding and encourage thoughtfulness around these actions. We are there to drip feed and seek 1% improvements, not revolutionise things!

This is a great theme to revisit at different points throughout a young person's time at school, ideally at least once a year while you have them for tutor time as this will help them to continually reflect on their actions and make sense of them.

Frequency
You may wish to incorporate this session on an annual basis and then have a check in and review after a time has passed.

96 Target setting

Resources: SMART sheet, pens/pencils
Preparation: five minutes to gather and distribute resources
Done well, target setting is a powerful process that can create opportunities for pupils to reflect upon their current results and abilities and actively plan for improvement. Rushed, or done without explicit guidance, and pupils can often write open wish lists that lack the short-term structure and steps to ensure them. Throughout the school year pupils should have the opportunity to create short- (proximal) and long-term (distal) targets, visit them regularly and update them. Target setting is often used as a low-level intervention with pupils who might be underperforming in key areas, or for example consistently missing the start of tutor time each morning. Working out targets together can be first step intervention here.

Instructions
With target setting it is best to follow a structured approach, to that end I recommend using SMART targets.

> Specific
> Measurable
> Achievable
> Realistic
> Time bound

Start by encouraging pupils to think about one key area of their school life they would like to improve and provide really clear examples, including 'learn the past participle rule for French', or 'be able to play three new songs on the keyboard', or 'practise quadratic equations until I feel more confident'.

Tutor time for academic improvement

AIMS AND GOALS PLANNER

AIMS AND GOALS

S — Specific — What exactly do you want to achieve?

M — Measurable — How will you track your advancement?

A — Attainable — Evaluate the feasibility of your goal.

R — Relevant — How does it fit into your broader objectives?

T — Time-bound — What is the deadline?

Break down your goal into 3 simple targets:

Target 1	Target 2	Target 3

Action Steps: Action Steps: Action Steps:

Image 5.1   Aims and Goals Template

The key here is to guide pupils not to go in for big bold goals, but to make them really specific and ideally measurable. Then going through each of the SMART areas, ask pupils to plot their approaches to achieving this target.

Discussion

Set aside regular time to revisit these targets and ensure pupils are encouraged to perfect their actions and outcome supports a positive environment where pupils can be supported towards meaningful improvements. Ideally, pupils should keep a record of their targets in tutor jotters or carefully filed documents for ease of access.

Frequency

You may wish to incorporate this session on an annual basis and then have a check in and review after a time has passed.

97 Metacognitive feedback reviews

Resources: None
Preparation: None

Metacognitive and self-regulation strategies encourage pupils to engage more actively with their learning by providing them with targeted techniques for planning, tracking and assessing their progress.

Throughout the year pupils will receive feedback, grades, reports and results to provide an overview of their progress in school to date. It is important to provide support and guidance to pupils so they are well placed to break this information down into usable information that can help with target setting, revision planning and forming a plan for improvement. Without support, improvement can feel daunting and insurmountable for pupils, especially those who study many subjects.

Instructions

Supporting pupils in thinking metacognitively about their feedback involves guiding them to reflect deeply and develop ownership over their progress.

Start by helping them see this feedback as a tool for improvement, rather than as a judgement on their performance. Encourage pupils to look for patterns in their feedback, are there recurring themes in areas like clarity, structure, grammar or detail?

Tutor time for academic improvement

Spotting these patterns allows them to target specific improvements, viewing feedback as connected steps towards progress. It can also help to prompt self-assessment before they receive external feedback, as this primes them to identify their strengths and areas for development more independently.

Introducing reflective questions such as 'What was my intention here?' or 'How could I approach this differently in the future?' helps them move beyond surface-level adjustments.

In addition, helping to translate feedback into tangible goals can make it feel more actionable; if they often struggle with structure, for example, they could set a goal to focus on clear introductions and conclusions in their next piece of work. Building in regular reflection time and encouraging the use of logs or tutor jotters, makes their progress more visible, and can reinforce the importance of reflection.

Discussion
Self-reflection, consolidation and acting on feedback is vital for pupils' success at school and after. Pupils with strong metacognitive skills are better equipped to gauge when they are confident in their knowledge within subjects, and when further study is needed. This should be done through self-awareness, test feedback and data from assessments; feelings alone are not the sole guide and with support from tutors as well as class teachers. The work of Townsend and Heit (2011) tells us clearly that pupils are not best placed to assess their own progress, and therefore need help to do it meaningfully, and Hacker and colleagues (2000) support this. Done well, this enables pupils to manage their time more effectively, dedicating appropriate time to each topic during revision.

Frequency
You may wish to incorporate this activity on an annual basis and then incorporate the target setting activities to support positive change.

98 Failure

Resources: none
Preparation: none
An important part of this process is to create a safe space for pupils to explore failure. A number of years ago I asked a group of senior pupils if they knew

what would happen if they failed a final exam (GCSE). One pupil said very confidently that you would have to retake the course next year and retake the exam. Another declared that you'd just cry, he said it would be awful and your embarrassment would bring tears quickly! A third said you would have to spend the next few years of school avoiding the teachers because they'd be very cross with you for failing their subject. When I thanked the pupils for offering these responses and offered them a more realistic version of what actually happens when a pupil fails an exam (not a great deal), or fails at something else in life, they were all surprised and relieved. Exploring failure with pupils doesn't make it more likely to happen, on the contrary, it provides a time and space to dispel the myths that can endure within schools and education.

 Instructions

It is best to do these sessions after a while when pupils know you well and feel comfortable asking questions, and do not feel that this discussion is a personal attack. These sessions might be more challenging for some pupils than others depending on their school successes to date, so be sensitive to that and avoid cold calling pupils as not everyone will feel comfortable talking about this openly.

I always start with mentioning my own experience of failure. I let pupils know that it took me more than one – and more than two – attempts to pass my driving test and we explore what happened next in my expensive journey to get behind the wheel! Then I explain to pupils that should they fail a final exam, the process is a little different to the driving test scenario. We discuss the possibility of an appeal, if that is within their exam system, and then talk about the emotional process and logistical one of moving on with their education. Importantly, I reassure pupils that they certainly will not need to expend energy hiding from their teachers!

The key thing to get across here is that within a life well lived, failure at one time or another is inevitable, and actually important for growth. For example, in 1991–1993 an ambitious – yet ill fated – ecological experiment took place in Arizona, USA. Biosphere 2 was designed to be a self-sustaining, closed-ssystem habitat, a kind of bubble where eight people known as *biospherians* were sealed. Among the many issues and problems was one interesting outcome for the trees: the trees in Biosphere 2 faced many challenges including one, unexpected challenge, they grew but could not develop the strength to stand on their own. This happened for a number of reasons, including the environment inside Biosphere 2 lacked the necessary wind to challenge and therefore strengthen

Tutor time for academic improvement

them. In short, the trees needed natural stress factors like wind, showing how integral they are to plant development. This anecdote is one I use often when discussing stress and worry with young people. Refer them back to the diagram on page 108 to ensure their stress and worry remain in the green zone.

 Discussion
The primary focus of this session is to dispel any mythology surrounding failure and provide pupils with answers to any queries they have and support them to plan for success with the safety of knowing the facts. Ideally, schools are able to ensure pupils are being assessed at the correct level and given the support to achieve success. Research indicates that when students are encouraged to learn from errors in a supportive environment; they are more likely to take intellectual risks, leading to deeper engagement and learning. However this requires active intervention and support as Eskreis-Winkler and colleagues (2024) suggest: the benefits of failure have been exaggerated. So it is important to keep this discussion based on the facts and likely outcomes for pupils exploring worse case scenarios without telling them about silver linings.

 Frequency
You may wish to incorporate this session in preparation for high-stakes assessment periods, it can work well alongside the activities on the following pages.

Sub-section 3: Strategies in action

99   Memory

Resources: the Image on Page 157
Preparation: none
Memory
In order to support pupils with their revision it is important to share some details of how their brain works, and what learning actually is. Explaining to pupils that learning creates a (usually positive) change to their brain in a physical sense can help pupils acknowledge why it can feel so difficult.

 Instructions
Using this diagram to explain to pupils both how learning happens, and why sometimes it does not, should provide some basis for them accepting the revision strategies that follow in the next few pages. To do this, share this

image on the board and explain that in order to learn we need to process information into our long-term memory. That process being when your consciousness, or attention, is given to something, that information is then placed into your finite, working memory, from there, depending on what you do next, it is either processed into your long-term memory and remembered, or forgotten. In order to take the information from your working memory, you need to do something, and preferably something that requires you to really think hard with it.

From there I explain to pupils that their ability to focus on the incoming information is based on a host of factors including the environment they're in and if there are avoidable distractions – phones and so on – near them, their own executive function and their mental state of wellbeing. Many of these can be improved with effort, habits and practise. From there, their working memory is not necessarily something that can be greatly improved, as we are born with a finite space to hold new information. The biggest opportunity here comes in the choice of learning activity and the ones on the next few pages are proven to be the most effective for ensuring hard thinking can be done.

Discussion

Of course there is a lot more to the brain and memory than detailed above, so your aim here is to provide a simplified version of what happens with the hope of establishing an understanding of why we need to undertake certain approaches to learning things. Explaining the memory in these very simplified terms should hopefully make them more receptive to changing their strategies from highlighting, summarising and rereading, to the more active approaches coming up.

 Frequency

This session is best delivered annually or biannually to effectively remind pupils of the importance of memory in their learning.

Retrieval

Teaching effective retrieval strategies is hugely impactful for revisions as it helps pupils to recall learned information from memory. As information is recalled from our memories, the memory is strengthened over time. The following strategies provide pupils with an opportunity to recall what they know and hopefully identify any gaps in their knowledge and understanding.

Tutor time for academic improvement

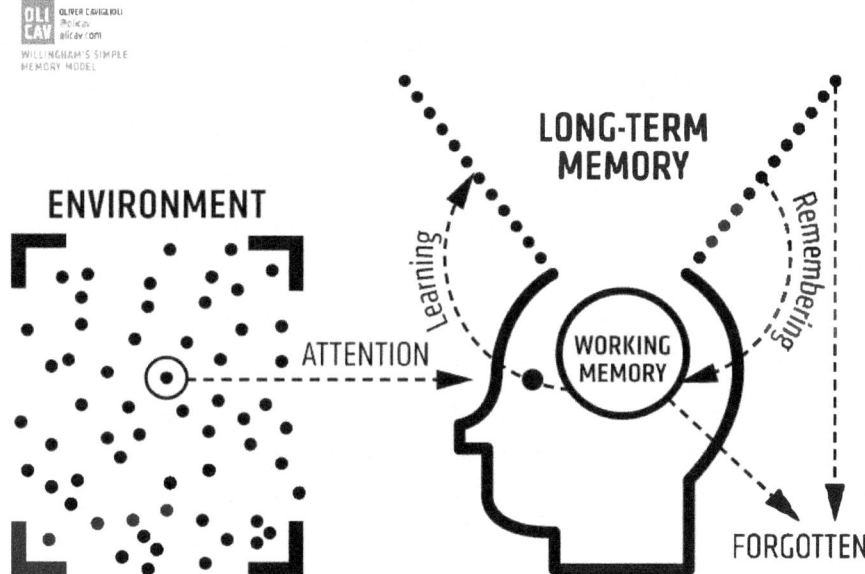

Image 5.2 Willingham's Simple Memory Model
Created by Oliver Caviglioli, with Nick Rose, Harry Fletcher-Wood and colleagues from the Institute for Teaching in winter 2019 (permissions grated kindly by @olicav).

Teaching pupils the theory of retrieval is a natural follow on from discussing the brain and memory as above. There are a number of strategies that support retrieval practice as detailed below. It is unlikely you will have time to fully engage with these strategies in tutor time so be wary not to take on too much, your primary aim is to expose your pupils to these strategies and help them to engage in them during their revision time. These are not sessions to be delivered in isolation but ones to be revised over time to provide sustained support for pupils. Consider checking and reviewing their approaches after these sessions is another good use of tutor time.

Flashcards

Take the time to teach pupils how to create effective flashcards that cover the topics they have been learning. Emphasise the importance of making structured, physical cards rather than using digital tools or apps. Explain that each card should have a question on one side and the correct answer on the other, which is crucial for promoting active recall, and ideally provide an example of a well-made flashcard so pupils can see this for themselves.

This hands-on approach not only reinforces learning but also engages them more deeply with the material. Explain to pupils that answering the question and then checking for accuracy is an important part of exercise that enables them to identify any misconceptions and gaps in their learning. Ideally they should take note of their scores so they can then re-examine their study plans depending on their success. Doing flashcards regularly will strengthen the connection between their subject memories and therefore make it easier to retrieve the information.

Quizzes

The creation and undertaking of quizzes created an ideal opportunity for pupils to test their recall and assess what they know about differently. Much like the flashcards above, this gives them the opportunity to find out what they are confident with, what they do not know and identify any misunderstandings. Stress to pupils that quizzes can be done with others, family members and peers. Your school might have preferred apps that support the creation of quizzes. Guide pupils to note down any areas for development and points to revisit in their learning and add this to their study plan to ensure they are fully engaging with the process to maximise their learning.

100 Teaching others

Resources: none
Preparation: none

Teaching this approach can easily be incorporated into your tutor time, especially before high-stakes assessments, where it may already occur naturally in tutor time. It is a useful and impactful strategy when done well. Socialising during study leave is essential for managing stress and supporting each other's wellbeing. Explain this to pupils and suggest that with some self-discipline, studying with friends is an effective overall strategy. Employing a framework by which to provide feedback to peers is a good way to ensure any feedback is effective, for example Berger (2003) suggests peer critique should be 'kind', 'specific' and 'helpful' is one way to support pupils to work together purposefully.

Encourage pupils to consider different ways they can teach each other key information ahead of high-stakes assessment. You can establish strategies which may include:

- taking 60 seconds each to cover the topics you need most comfortable with;
- noting down two correct pieces of information and one mistake for your peers;
- adding further details into an answer written by your peer and then explaining your thinking;
- or for creative content, role play may be suitable;
- giving each other instructions for improving an answer or piece of work.

Encourage pupils to ask their peers 'how' and 'why' questions and engage in elaborative interrogation which encourages them to explore other answers and justify their thoughts as this will expand their thinking and make it a little harder for them, which ensures active thinking is taking place!

101 Brain dump

Resources: paper, pens/pencils
Preparation: none
The brain dump is an effective revision strategy that allows pupils to consolidate their learning by writing down everything they know about a topic. This can be done to establish what they need to learn, and what gaps exist, or to identify how successful their revision to date has been. Explain to pupils that this is best done under time conditions so it does not become too open-ended. Advise pupils that they will need paper and to set their timer for around ten minutes. Ideally, for reasons mentioned above, this should be done as much as possible in a distraction-free environment. After completing the dump, they can use their notes to check over their work and to elaborate on key concepts, and reflect on their understanding to enhance retention and learning. Or suggest to pupils that asking a class teacher to check over their work will provide further feedback and support to direct their learning.

102 Mind mapping

Resources: creative resources, paper, pens
Preparation: five minutes to collect and distribute resources
Mind mapping is an incredibly effective method for supporting the creation of long-term memory and enhancing learning. Guiding pupils in this technique

requires dedicated time and attention to ensure it is done correctly and pupils do not end up working on spider diagrams which are much less effective. Mind mapping encourages pupils to record their knowledge in multiple ways, employing dual coding to incorporate various modalities and maximise the brain's capacity to process information. Provide pupils with clear examples, which can be found via a quick google, discuss the use of **phrases, words, images and colour** and encourage pupils to note down their own set of instructions or make a mind map. If you decided to encourage pupils to create mind maps in tutor time this may take a number of sessions to ensure all elements are included.

103 Deliberate practise

Resources: access to the internet to show pupils where to find past paper questions
Preparation: none

This session aims to equip you with strategies to guide effective revision, keeping in mind that launching full-scale revision within tutor time may be too ambitious. Instead, start by providing a simple framework for setting up revision practices. I recommend deliberate practice as a method pupils can use once they are comfortable with their knowledge base. This approach requires focused effort to express their understanding in the format required for their high-stakes assessments. Encourage pupils to approach these activities only when they are confident about the learning outcomes.

Any practice they undertake should be challenging, though it does not need to be without support; they can use basic notes, extended time or guides which can be gradually removed. This helps them stay in the *Goldilocks zone* of difficulty, neither too easy nor too hard but, as Goldilocks would say, 'just right!'. Feedback is essential in deliberate practice, so encourage pupils to review their work with the outcomes or in consultation with their classroom teacher, to refine and deepen their understanding.

 Frequency

The wonderful thing about offering a variety of options for pupils to explore in this section is how easy it is to mix and match, allowing for a diverse range of activities throughout the calendar year. Involving pupils in scheduling these sessions not only provides them with a sense of autonomy but also ensures the approach is responsive to their needs.

Final thoughts

Ensuring pupils have a positive start to the day, where they are met by someone who knows them and recognises their achievements and challenges is a sensible way to support a positive school culture. Routines are essential for encouraging good habits and cultivating positive school cultures in numerous ways, they establish consistency and predictability within the school environment, fostering a sense of stability and security among pupils, teachers and staff. Tutor Time also helps communicate and underpin the wider values of the school community through the sharing of values and discussion relating to and challenges, changes or developments in school rules, values and structure. It offers space and guidance to reflect on previous behaviours and actively plan together for improvement.

The theory of *distributed practice*, or the *little and often* approach is one what we can activate here for excellent outcomes. This theory has been widely written about in many other disciplines including sport, chess and creative endeavours. The research on distributed practice by Gerbier and Toppino (2015) argues that engaging in frequent, shorter sessions of focused work supports stronger retention, deeper understanding and skill mastery compared to longer, infrequent sessions. This not only highlights the case for spaced practice in academic revision methods, but I believe also strengthens the case for ensuring that the tutor time curriculum is designed and is purposeful in setting out its aims in line with the wider school aims. Through regular, daily reminders, support and discussion, all schools have a powerful channel to improve whole-school outcomes.

Stephen Curry, an NBA basketball player, is an excellent example of someone who uses distributed practice to master his skills practising his shooting accuracy through brief, daily practice rather than exhaustive drills. This strategy allows him to build muscle memory without the fatigue that can reduce learning quality. Chess master Magnus Carlsen is another example of a high achiever who has pursued shorter, regular sessions over integrity to hone his abilities and skills.

In schools, adopting a similar model in spending just 15 minutes each day on thoughtfully designed activities can provide the mental prompts and opportunities to improve and develop skills, knowledge and abilities. Whether it is maths, routines or revision, these short, consistent sessions allow pupils to reinforce their understanding of how to manage the challenges and expectations of school life and life in general.

'We are what we repeatedly do. Excellence, then, is not an act, but a habit'. This well-known quote, often attributed to Aristotle, but actually written by Will Durant, is nonetheless a powerful reminder that if we want positive outcomes in schools, creating space to regularly focus on wellbeing, culture and study strategies is an excellent place to start.

Crucially, we must acknowledge the significant amount of time dedicated to tutor time. If just 10 minutes a day is allocated four times a week, this amounts to nearly 33 hours per year. If 20 minutes is spent four times a week, this rises to an impressive 65 hours annually. Rather than viewing these sessions in isolation, we should recognise them as part of a broader, structured programme. When approached strategically, this time presents a valuable opportunity for schools, leaders, and pupils to make meaningful progress in various aspects of school life.

Remember, the tortoise won the race, not the hare. In education we have to fight hard against shiny, new and exciting interventions that lack the rigour of proof. Our time should be spent cementing and reinforcing the foundations of school life. Using this book to develop your tutor time curriculum will be particularly impactful when each activity supports long-term school goals, creating an incremental yet powerful pathway to school success.

References

Ambitious about Autism. (2022). Compelling attendance won't result in more autistic pupils in school. www.ambitiousaboutautism.org.uk/about-us/media-centre/news/compelling-attendance-wont-result-more-autistic-pupils-school

Arslan, G. (2021). School belongingness, well-being, and mental health among adolescents: Exploring the role of loneliness. *Australian Journal of Psychology*, 73(1), 70–80. https://doi.org/10.1080/00049530.2021.1904499

Berger, R. (2003). *An Ethic of Excellence*. Portsmouth, NH: Heinemann.

Bus, A.G., Shang, Y. and Roskos, K. (2024). Building a stronger case for independent reading at school. *AERA Open, 10*. https://doi.org/10.1177/23328584241267843

Cain, N. and Gradisar, M. (2020). Electronic media use and sleep in school-aged children and adolescents: A review. *Sleep Medicine*, 11(8), 735–742. https://doi.org/10.1016/j.sleep.2010.02.006

Carvalho, P.F. and Goldstone, R.L. (2015). The benefits of interleaved and blocked study: Different tasks benefit from different schedules of study. *Psychonomic Bulletin & Review*, 22(1), 281–288.

Clear, J. (2018). *Atomic Habits*. Cornerstone Digital.

Connolly, S. and Mullally, S. (2022). School distress in UK school children: The parental lived experience. doi: https://doi.org/10.1101/2023.02.16.23286034

Cooper, K.M., Haney, B., Krieg, A. and Brownell, S.E. (2017). What's in a name? The importance of students perceiving that an instructor knows their names in a high-enrollment biology classroom. *CBE: Life Sciences Education*, 16(1). https://doi.org/10.1187/cbe.16-08-0265

Cornelius-White, J. (2007). Learner-centered teacher-student relationships are effective: A Meta-analysis. *Review of Educational Research*, 77(1),113–143.

Cosma, A., Stevens, G., Martin et al. (2020). Cross-national time trends in adolescent mental well-being from 2002 to 2018 and the explanatory role of schoolwork pressure. *Journal of Adolescent Health*, 66(6S): S50–S58. doi: 10.1016/j.jadohealth.2020.02.010.

Englund, R.L., Graham, R.J. and Dinsmore, P.C. (2003). *Creating the Project Office*. Jossey-Bass.

Duhugg, C. (2014). *The Power of Habit: Why We Do What We Do in Life and Business*. Random House.

Dunlosky, J., Rawson, K.A., Marsh, E.J. et al. (2013). Improving students' learning with effective learning techniques: Promising directions from cognitive and

References

educational psychology. *Psychological Science in the Public Interest, 14*(1), 4–58. doi: 10.1177/1529100612453266

Eskreis-Winkler, L., Woolley, K., Erensoy, E. and Kim, M. (2024). The exaggerated benefits of failure. *Journal of Experimental Psychology: General, 153*(7): 1920–1937. doi: 10.1037/xge0001610.

Fogg, B.J. (2019). *Tiny Habits: The Small Changes That Change Everything*. Virgin Digital.

Gerbier, C. and Toppino, T.C. (2015). The effect of distributed practice: Neuroscience, cognition, and education, *Trends in Neuroscience and Education, 4*(3), 49–59. https://doi.org/10.1016/j.tine.2015.01.001

Glass, B. (2019). House system: Increasing community, motivation, and student ownership. *Masters of Education in Teaching and Learning*, 14. https://digitalcommons.acu.edu/metl/14

The Children's Society (2024). The Good Childhood Report. www.childrenssociety.org.uk/sites/default/files/2020-11/Good-Childhood-Report-2020.pdf

Hacker, D.J., Bol, L., Horgan, D.D. and Rakow, E.A. (2000). Test prediction and performance in a classroom context. *Journal of Educational Psychology, 92*(1), 160–170. https://doi.org/10.1037/0022-0663.92.1.160

Högberg, B. (2021). Educational stressors and secular trends in school stress and mental health problems in adolescents. *Social Science and Medicine, 270*, 113616. doi: 10.1016/j.socscimed.2020.113616

Hattie, J. (2003). Teachers make a difference: What is the research evidence? Paper presented at the Building Teacher Quality: What Does the Research Tell Us Australian Council for Educational Research Conference. http://research.acer.edu.au/research_conference_2003/4/

Hattie, J. (2009). *Visible Learning: A Synthesis of Over 800 Meta-Analyses Relating to Achievement*. Routledge.

Jindal-Snape, D. and Cantali, D. (2019). A four-stage longitudinal study exploring pupils' experiences, preparation and support systems during primary–secondary school transitions. *British Educational Research Journal*. doi:10.1002/berj.3561

Jindal-Snape, D., Bradshaw, P., Gilbert, A. et al. (2023). Primary–secondary school transition experiences and factors associated with differences in these experiences: Analysis of the longitudinal Growing Up in Scotland dataset. *Review of Education, 11*(3), Article e3444. https://doi.org/10.1002/rev3.3444

Karpicke, J. and Blunt, J. (2011). Retrieval practice produces more learning than elaborative studying with concept mapping. *Science, 331*, 772–775.

Kirschner, P.A., Sweller, J. and Clark, R.E. (2006). Why minimal guidance during instruction does not work: An analysis of the failure of constructivist, discovery, problem-based, experiential, and inquiry-based teaching. *Educational Psychologist, 41*(2), 75–86. https://doi.org/10.1207/s15326985ep4102_1

Kuyken, W., Ball, S., Crane, C., et al. and MYRIAD Team Group. (2022). Effectiveness and cost-effectiveness of universal school-based mindfulness training compared with normal school provision in reducing risk of mental health problems and promoting well-being in adolescence: the MYRIAD cluster randomised controlled trial. *BMJ Evidence-Based Mental Health*, 25(3), 99–109. http://dx.doi.org/10.1136/ebmental-2021-300396

Lewin, K. (1942). Field theory and learning. *Teachers College Record*, 43(10), 215–242. https://doi.org/10.1177/016146814204301006

Office for National Statistics (ONS). (2021). Special Educational Needs in England. https://explore-education-statistics.service.gov.uk/find-statistics/special-educational-needs-inengland/2020-21

Padilla-Walker, L.M., Hardy, S.A. and Christensen, K.J. (2011). Adolescent hope as a mediator between parent-child connectedness and adolescent outcomes. *The Journal of Early Adolescence*, 31(6), 853–879. https://doi.org/10.1177/0272431610376249

Pan, S.C. and Rickard, T.C. (2018). Transfer of test-enhanced learning: Meta-analytic review and synthesis. *Psychological Bulletin*, 144(7), 627–656.

Pearson, N., Sherar, L.B. and Hamer, M. (2019). Prevalence and correlates of meeting sleep, screen-time, and physical activity guidelines among adolescents in the United Kingdom. *JAMA Pediatrics*, 173(10), 993–994.

PISA publications | OECD

Roorda, D.L., Koomen, H.M.Y., Spilt, J.L. and Oort, F.J. (2011). The influence of affective teacher–student relationships on students' school engagement and achievement: A meta-analytic approach. *Review of Educational Research*, 81(4), 493–529.

Slater, M.D., Johnson, B.K., Cohen, J. et al. (2014). Temporarily expanding the boundaries of the self: Motivations for entering the story world and implications for narrative effects. *Journal of Communication*, 64(3), 439–455. doi: https://doi.org/10.1111/jcom.12100

Taylor, K. and Rohrer, D. (2010). The effects of interleaved practice. *Applied Cognitive Psychology*, 24(6), 837–848.

Tononi, G. and Cirelli, C. (2003). Sleep and synaptic homeostasis: A hypothesis. *Brain Research Bulletin*, 62, 143–150.

Townsend, C.L. and Heit, E. (2011). Judgments of learning and improvement. *Memory & Cognition*, 39(2), 204–216. doi: 10.3758/s13421-010-0019-2

Twenge, J.M. and Campbell, W.K. (2018). Associations between screen time and lower psychological well-being among children and adolescents: Evidence from a population-based study. Preventive Medicine Reports, 18(12), 271–283. doi: 10.1016/j.pmedr.2018.10.003

Walton, G.M., Cohen, G.L., Cwir, D. and Spencer, S.J. (2012) Mere belonging: The power of social connections. *Journal of Personality and Social Psychology*, 102(3), 513–532.

West, P., Sweeting, H. and Young, R. (2010). Transition matters: Pupils' experiences of the primary–secondary school transition in the West of Scotland and consequences for well-being and attainment. *Research Papers in Education*, 25(1), 21–50. https://doi.org/10.1080/02671520802308677

Willingham, D. (2012). *When Can You Trust the Experts? How to Tell Good Science from Bad in Education*. Josey-Bass.

Index

Absurdle 77
academic improvement, activities for 15; academic interventions 135–145; brain dump 159; check-ins, organisational 143–144; deliberate practice 160; effective techniques 132–135; exams 145; memory 155–158; mind mapping 159–160; numeracy interventions 140–142; reading programmes 136–138; retrieval strategies 156–158; revision planning 136, 146–155; SEND support 142–144; spelling 138–139; strategies in action 136, 155–160; teaching others 158–159; typing practice 145
activities *see* academic improvement, activities for; Annual Observations and Celebrations; health and wellbeing activities; school culture and community; transition from primary to secondary schools
age, mixed, in groups 32–33
aggregation of marginal gains 36–38
aims and goals planner 151
Allergy Awareness Week 96
alternatives to tutor time 27–30
anagram challenge 139
animals: National Pet Month 95–96; World Animal Day 85
Annual Observations and Celebrations: Allergy Awareness Week 96; Anti-Bullying Week 87; April 94–96; Armistice 86–87; Black History Month 84; Brain Awareness Week 93; community/wider society 79; December 87–88; Energy Saving Week 89; February 91–92; history of 92–93; International Day of Charity 81–82; International Day of Peace 83; International Day of Persons with Disabilities 88; January 88–91; June 98–100; looking ahead to 75–76; Lunar New Year 89–90; March 92–94; Martin Luther King Day 90–91; May 96–98; Mental Health Awareness Week 95; National Fitness Day 82–83; National Pet Month 95–96; National Poetry Day 94; National Walking Month 97–98; Neurodiversity Celebration Week 94; November 86–87; October 83–86; Pride Month 98–99; progress reports, reviews of 91; Refugee Week 99–100; research, into new topics by students, drawbacks of 80; Safer Internet Day 92; September 80–83; Sports Personality of the Year 88; Thank a Teacher Day 100; World Animal Day 85; World Letter Writing Day 81; World Space Week 84–85; World Wildlife Day 93
Anti-Bullying Week 87
anxiety, avoiding use of term 106–107
April, events in 94–96
Armistice 86–87
Arslan, G. 33, 64
Artle 77
assemblies 67–68
attendance 18–20, 24
audits of tutor time 30
automatic doors 26, 143–144
autonomy: students 19–20; teachers 11–12

behaviour management: Anti-Bullying Week 87; assemblies 67–68; environment for tutor time 24–27; norms, communication of 64–69; sanctions 69–70; sensory load 26–27; tutor time and 30

Index

belonging, sense of 63, 64
Berger, R. 158
Bezos, J. 1, 5
bingo games 54–55, 56
birthday list 58–59
Black History Month 84
Blunt, J. 134
Brailsford, D. 36–38
Brain Awareness Week 93
brain dump 159
brains: memory and 155–158; multitasking and 130; physical health and 125; sensory load 26–27; sleep and 118
buddy systems 32–33
bullying - Anti-Bullying Week 87
Bus, A.G. 137

calendars, managing 71–73
Cantali, D. 8
captains 33
Carlsen, M. 161–162
charities 81–82
check-ins: organisational 143–144; wellbeing 104–106
Children's Mental Health Week 91–92
Childsmile 6–7
Cirelli, C. 118
Clark, R.E. 80
co-curricular activities 63–64
collaborative drawing 52–54
competence of students 19–20
connectedness 64
consistency of tutors 29–30
consultation with teachers 4
Cornelius-White, J. 28
Cosma, A. 132
Countdown TV challenge 142
Crosswordle 77
crosswords 138
Curry, S. 161

daily maths challenge 141–142
daily time, organisation of: calendars 71–73; equipment 73–75
data analysis mini task 141
December, events in 87–88
Deci, E. 19
deliberate practice 160
design of tutor time curriculum 14; school improvement planning 38–43; small changes, impact of 36–38

diaries: homework diaries/planners 20–21; sleep 119–122
digital distractions, managing 129–131
Dinsmore, P.C. 128
disability - International Day of Persons with Disabilities 88
distributed practice 133, 161–162
Dordle 77
Dunlosky, J. 133
Durant, W. 162

Edmondson, A. 19–20
elaborative interrogation 133
Energy Saving Week 89
Englund, R.L. 128
environment for tutor time 24–27
equipment, organisation of 73–75
e-safety 92
events *see* Annual Observations and Celebrations
exams 145; failure, exploration of 153–155
exercises *see* academic improvement, activities for; Annual Observations and Celebrations; health and wellbeing activities; school culture and community; transition from primary to secondary schools
expectations: communication of 64–69; sanctions 69–70
extra-curricular activities 63–64

failure, exploration of 153–155
familiarity effect 34–35
February, events in 91–92
feedback: reflecting and acting on by students 152–153; from students 127–128
field theory 25–26
fitness: National Fitness Day 82–83; National Walking Month 97–98
flashcards 157–158
friendships 53–54
fun sessions 76–79

games for fun 76–79
Gerbier, C. 161
getting to know each other bingo 54–55, 56
Graham, R.J. 128
gratitude 128–129
Great Wind Blows 51–52

167

Index

habit forming 148–150
habit-stacking 38–39
handwriting 81
Hattie, J. 29
health and wellbeing activities 15; check-in 104–106; digital distractions, managing 129–131; feedback from students 127–128; gratitude 128–129; grief 116–117; hope/hopefulness 108–111; mental health 112–113; physical health 124–126; sign posting help 126–127; sleep 117–124; stress and worry, discussions about 106–108; to-do lists 114–116; workload check 111–112; world events, responding to 116–117
Heit, E. 153
help, seeking 126–127
Högberg, B. 132
homework diaries/planners 20–21
hope/hopefulness 108–111
house systems 31–34
house time 62–63

icebreakers: birthday list 58–59; collaborative drawing 52–54; getting to know each other bingo 54–55, 56; Great Wind Blows 51–52; Jenga question and answer 49–50; marshmallow/Starburst Challenge 50–51; name cards 47; riddles 48–49; Spot Light 59–61; this or that 55, 57–58
identity, creating a sense of 64
innate sense of students' needs 29–30
inter-house competitions 33
interleaved practice 133–134, 147–148
International Day of Charity 81–82
International Day of Peace 83
International Day of Persons with Disabilities 88
internet - Safer Internet Day 92
Isaac, A. 45
IYKYK 77

January, events in 88–91
Jenga question and answer 49–50
Jindal-Snape, D. 8
June, events in 98–100

Karpicke, J. 134
King, M.L. - Martin Luther King Day 90–91
Kirschner, P.A. 80

leadership, house system and 33
learning, sleep and 118–119
letter writing 81
Lewin, K. 25
LGBTQ+ community - Pride Month 98–99
literacy interventions 30, 136–138
little and often approach 161–162
logistics of tutor time 13–14; alternatives to tutor time 27–30; attendance 18–20; consistency of tutors 29–30; differences between schools 16, 17; environment for tutor time 24–27; quality assurance for tutor time 17; record keeping 18; removal of tutor time, impact of 22–24; sensory load 26–27; time allocations 17
long-term memory 156, 157
Lunar New Year 89–90

March, events in 92–94
marshmallow challenge 50–51
Martin Luther King Day 90–91
May, events in 96–98
memory 118–119, 155–158
mental health: check-in 104–106; Children's Mental Health Week 91–92; gratitude 128–129; hope/hopefulness 108–111; Mental Health Awareness Week 95; school work pressure 132; stress and worry, discussions about 106–108; World Mental Health Day 85–86
mental maths 140
mental training and preparation *see* transition from primary to secondary schools
mentoring, house system and 32–33
mere exposure effect 34–35
metacognitive feedback reviews 152–153
micro-actions 36–38
mind mapping 159–160
mindset of teachers, recommendations for 3
mixed age groups 32–33
mobile phones, e-safety and 92
'Mona Lisa' (Da Vinci) painting 27–28
motivation of pupils 19–20
Myatt, M. 30

Index

name cards 47
names of children, learning and using 46
National Fitness Day 82–83
National Pet Month 95–96
National Poetry Day 94
National Walking Month 97–98
needs, psychological 19–20
needs-based organisation of groups 34
negative habits 149
Nerdle 77
neurodivergent pupils 21
Neurodiversity Celebration Week 94
neuroscience - Brain Awareness Week 93
norms: communication of 64–69; sanctions 69–70
November, events in 86–87
number line completion 141
numeracy interventions 140–142

October, events in 83–86
Octordle 78
Odd Socks Day 87
1% rule 36–38
oral health of children 6–7
organisation: academic responsibilities of students 20–22; daily checks 143; equipment 73–75; SEND 21; time 71–73

Pan, S.C. 147–148
pastoral leads 8–9
peace - International Day of Peace 83
peer teaching 158–159
percentage conversion practice 141
personal assistants, tutor teachers as 10
pets - National Pet Month 95–96
physical health 124–126; National Fitness Day 82–83; National Walking Month 97–98
planning: calendars 71–73; equipment, organisation of 73–75; homework diaries/planners 20–21; Whole-School Improvement Plans 39–43
positive stress 107
practice testing 133, 134
prefects 33
preparation for school transition *see* transition from primary to secondary schools
presentations 59–61
Pride Month 98–99

primary-secondary school transition *see* transition from primary to secondary schools
primary teacher relationship, loss of 8
problem-solving, real-world 140
progress reports, reviews of 91
psychological needs/safety 19–20
public speaking skills 59–61
pupil feedback 127–128
pupil-teacher relationships 3, 8, 10, 18, 28–29, 65

quality assurance for tutor time 17
quizzes 158
Quordle 78

reading programmes 136–138
real-world problem-solving 140
Refugee Week 99–100
relatedness, students and 19–20
removal of tutor time, impact of 22–24
research: being informed by 3; into new topics by students, drawbacks of 80
responsibilities of teachers 11–12
retrieval strategies 156–158
reviews of tutor time 30
revision: brain dump 159; deliberate practice 160; effective techniques 132–135; failure, exploration of 153–155; habit forming 148–150; interleaved practice 147–148; memory 155–158; metacognitive feedback reviews 152–153; mind mapping 159–160; planning 136, 146–155; target setting 150–152; teaching others 158–159
Rickard, T.C. 147–148
riddles 48–49
Rohrer, D. 147
room allocation for tutor time 24–27
Rooney, W. 45
Roorda, D.L. 28–29
Roskos, K. 137
routine inductions 64–67
routines, establishing 143, 144–145
Ryan, R. 19

Safer Internet Day 92
safety, psychological 19–20
sanctions 69–70
school culture and community 14; assemblies 67–68; birthday list 58–59; collaborative drawing 52–54;

Index

difficulties with 44; equipment, organisation of 73–75; expectations, communication of 64–69; extra-curricular activities 63–64; fun sessions 76–79; getting to know each other bingo 54–55, 56; Great Wind Blows 51–52; house time 62–63; Jenga question and answer 49–50; marshmallow/Starburst Challenge 50–51; mental training and preparation 45–46; name cards 47; names of children, learning and using 46, 47; riddles 48–49; routine inductions 64–67; sanctions 69–70; school events, looking ahead to 75–76; Spot Light 59–61; this or that 55, 57–58; time, organisation of 71–73; *see also* Annual Observations and Celebrations
school events, looking ahead to 75–76; *see also* Annual Observations and Celebrations
school improvement planning 38–43
school work pressure 132
screen time 129–131
Self-Determination Theory (SDT) 19–20
self-explanation 133
self-regulation strategies 152–153
self-testing 133
SEND support 21, 34, 142–144
sensory load 26–27
September, events in 80–83
Shang, Y. 137
sign posting help 126–127
sleep: diaries 119–122; hygiene, improving 122–124; importance of 117–119, 121–122; learning and memory and 118–119
small changes, impact of 36–38
SMART targets 150–152
social and behavioural norms: communication of 64–69; sanctions 69–70
social connections, building 53–54
social prescriptions 63
spaced learning 133, 134
space - World Space Week 84–85
Special Educational Needs and Disabilities (SEND) support 21, 34, 142–144
specialisation, organisation of groups by 34
spelling activities 138–139

spelling word race 138
Sporcle 78
sports: National Fitness Day 82–83; Sports Personality of the Year 88
Spot Light 59–61
spot the mistakes 139
Starburst Challenge 50–51
stress and worry: discussions about 106–108; school work pressure 132
structure for tutor time 12–13, 30–35
student feedback 127–128
study techniques 132–135
support, seeking 126–127
Sweller, J. 80

target setting 150–152
task management 114–116
Taylor, K. 147
teacher-pupil relationships 3, 8, 10, 18, 28–29, 65
teachers: autonomy and responsibilities of 11–12; consultation with 4; Thank a Teacher Day 100
Teacher Tapp 4–5
teaching, peer 158–159
Thank a Teacher Day 100
Think-Pair-Share 86
this or that 55, 57–58
time: allocation for tutor time 17; organisation of 71–73, 114–116
times tables 140
timetables: exam 143; visual displays of 143
to-do lists 114–116
tolerable stress 107
Tononi, G. 118
Toppino, T.C. 161
Townsend, C.L. 153
toxic stress 107
Tradle 78
transition from primary to secondary schools: assemblies 67–68; birthday list 58–59; collaborative drawing 52–54; difficulties with 44; equipment, organisation of 73–75; expectations, communication of 64–69; extra-curricular activities 63–64; fun sessions 76–79; getting to know each other bingo 54–55, 56; Great Wind Blows 51–52; house time 62–63; Jenga question and answer 49–50; marshmallow/Starburst Challenge 50–51; mental

training and preparation 45–46; name cards 47; names of children, learning and using 46, 47; riddles 48–49; routine inductions 64–67; sanctions 69–70; school events, looking ahead to 75–76; Spot Light 59–61; this or that 55, 57–58; time, organisation of 71–73
tutor groups, allocation to 31–35
tutor teachers: as first point of contact 22; meaningful 8–10; as personal assistants 10; role of 3
tutor time: benefits of 27–28; defined 2–3; distributed practice, theory of 161–162; inconsistency in approach to 5; removal of, impact of 22–24; reviews of 30; SEND support and 143–144; structure for 12–13; as unique but overlooked 5; value of 6, 161; wider school aims and 12; *see also* design of tutor time curriculum; logistics of tutor time
Tutor Time activities *see* academic improvement, activities for; Annual Observations and Celebrations; health and wellbeing; school culture and community; transition from primary to secondary schools
typing practice 145

value of tutor time 6
values of the school community 10
vertical tutor groups systems 32–33
voice, pupil 127–128

walking - National Walking Month 97–98

wellbeing, emotional, physical and academic 15; check-in 104–106; Childsmile 6–7; consistent contact with main teacher 7–8; digital distractions, managing 129–131; feedback from students 127–128; gratitude 128–129; grief 116–117; hope/hopefulness 108–111; mental health 112–113; National Walking Month 97–98; physical health 124–126; power of schools 7; sign posting help 126–127; sleep 117–124; stress and worry, discussions about 106–108; to-do lists 114–116; workload check 111–112; world events, responding to 116–117
Whole-School Improvement Plans 39–43
'why' questions, asking 133
wildlife - World Wildlife Day 93
Willingham, D. 3
Wizarding Wordle 78
word building challenge 139
workload: check 111–112; management of 114–116
World Animal Day 85
Worldle 78
World Letter Writing Day 81
World Mental Health Day 85–86
World Space Week 84–85
World Wildlife Day 93
worries: discussions about 106–108; school work pressure 132

Yerkes-Dodson curve 108

For Product Safety Concerns and Information please contact our EU representative GPSR@taylorandfrancis.com
Taylor & Francis Verlag GmbH, Kaufingerstraße 24, 80331 München, Germany